THE FALL OF AN AMERICAN ROME

The Fall of an American Rome

De-Industrialization of the American Dream

Quentin R. Skrabec Jr.

Algora Publishing
New York

Library of Congress Cataloging-in-Publication Data —

Skrabec, Quentin R.
    The fall of an American Rome: deindustrialization of the American dream / Quentin
R. Skrabec Jr.
        pages cm
    Includes bibliographical references and index.
    ISBN 978-1-62894-060-2 (soft cover: alk. paper) — ISBN 978-1-62894-061-9 (hard
cover: alk. paper) — ISBN 978-1-62894-062-6 (ebook) 1. Deindustrialization—United
States. 2. United States—Economic policy—21st century. 3. United States—Economic
conditions—21st century. I. Title.
    HD5708.55.U6S57 2014
    338.973—dc23
                                2013049449

Printed in the United States

To Our Lady of Walsingham and my father, Quentin, Sr., who rests
with her awaiting the return of American manufacturing.

Table of Contents

PREFACE

> In passing along the highway one frequently sees large and spacious build-
> ings, with the glass broken out the windows, the shutters hanging in ru-
> inous disorder, without any appearance of activity and enveloped in soli-
> tary gloom. Upon inquiry what they are, you are almost always informed
> that they were some cotton or other factory, which their proprietors
> could no longer keep in motion against overwhelming pressure of foreign
> competition.
>
> — Henry Clay, 1820, in his founding of the Whig Party and American
> System

This is the story of the de-industrialization of America. It tries to tell
the story based on the facts, not from a political viewpoint — which is
not as difficult as it may seem, since both American political parties support free trade economics. Nor does it try to center the responsibility on
the union, the workers, management, politicians, or even the American
public, since there is plenty of blame to share. Even the economic policy
of the country since 1945, which clearly must carry a large portion of the
blame, was accepted for all the right reasons. Free trade was expected to
promote world peace and democracy. No one foresaw what the ancillary
effects on the United States would be by the 1970s. To this end, I hope
to show the destruction on our cities, workers, managers, and country.
As far as blame, I have excluded no one from suspicion for we all are to
blame. I have found no villains or conspiracies, at least not of the "black
helicopter" type. In fact, our misguided polices have been for altruistic
goals most of the time.

There is no political viewpoint since both parties have part of the answer. The polarization in American politics has left the government unable to map out a true manufacturing policy for the nation. Union and non-union politics have taken priority over a national solution. As to economic approaches, both parties have adopted a free trade approach. Polarization has made us incapable of compromise on environmental issues. Politicians have, more than not, mined the de-industrialization of America for votes versus solving the problem. Citizens have been left to watch the unfolding de-industrialization, not sure what's going wrong or understanding why.

If there is a viewpoint, it is one of a love for American manufacturing and those American cities such as Detroit, Toledo, Pittsburgh, Akron, and so many others. I lived in and worked in the industrial burghs of Pittsburgh, Cleveland, Akron, Detroit, Toledo, Braddock, Canton, and Weirton. I grew up in the steel city of Pittsburgh and loved its manufacturing environment. My dad was a manufacturing manager; my grandfather was a steelworker; my great grandfather a steel engineer. My uncles worked in the mills, as did most of the parents of my friends. I played on steel slag dumps, attended the great annual steelworker Christmas parties for kids, and found hope in the industrial philanthropies such as the Carnegie Library and Museum. I lived happily in the "dirty" industrial ghetto of the "Mon" Valley, not realizing how bad I was having it. The same steel industry that put mill dust on the porch and smoke in the air everyday also gave me access to the world's best libraries and museums. In fact, with all the dirt, smoke, and labor struggles, the mills contributed to the happiest days of my life.

I went on to major in engineering at the University of Michigan, finding a passion for manufacturing. Near Ann Arbor is The Henry Ford Museum and Greenfield Village, where I still find inspiration and peace. I returned to Pittsburgh and the steel industry (again happily). I had a career working with various steel and auto suppliers. I gained a unique global perspective, having been a manager in a steel joint venture of America's #2 and Japan's #2 steelmakers in LTV and Sumitomo. I learned from the inside the attack of Japanese steel and automakers on the American market.

In the 1980s I would experience firsthand one of the nation's largest steel mergers, and a few years later one of its largest bankruptcies. As the manufacturing base collapsed in America, I left industry to obtain a PhD in manufacturing. Initially, I hoped to help drive a manufacturing revolution with such programs as Lean Manufacturing, Six Sigma, and

ISO 9000. This type of program, while extremely helpful to industry, was unable to overcome the political and economic infrastructure in America today. We have a policy of de-industrialization, although no one refers to it that way. Instead we are told of a post-industrial strategy where information will be the source of jobs. Still, I believed manufacturing could be saved.

As industry collapsed, it left few opportunities; I turned my research to the rise, decline, and the potential renaissance of American industry. I have published much of its history including a literary pantheon of great American industrialists. Now it is time to move to understanding the decline so we can have a renaissance. I have avoided this book because there is hurt and pain in the memories of industrial America. For some, this will be hard to understand. I feel sad driving past old factories. I even miss the dirt, because in Pittsburgh, mill dust in the morning dew was a sign of prosperity. I loved the smell of sulfur in the air, for it too came in times of great prosperity. These strange linkages were industrial signs of a bountiful Christmas for a child in Pittsburgh. I spent hours as a child on hills watching coal barges on the river, endless trains, and the beautiful orange glow of the night skies. I've seen the aurora borealis, but it does not compare to the night sky of Pittsburgh in 1958. For someone who has lived in the country all their lives, living in industrial Pittsburgh of the 1960s would seem like hell, not heaven. One can have the same love for the old wonder of an industrial city as many have for a white sand beach in the Bahamas.

For years as I managed the melt shop of the steel industry, there was always a joy and a fear in seeing hot liquid steel; there was a beauty also. Nights in the melt shop were awe inspiring. Using high powered electric furnaces to melt steel is a true triumph of modern man. Nothing in my memory is as vivid as my nights in the melt shop. It was also an explanation for the glowing orange skies of my childhood in Pittsburgh. There was a sense of power in being part of those orange skies. Industry can have a beauty that few realize.

Look at the art of Diego Rivera in Detroit or the art of John White Alexander on the walls of the Carnegie Museum. The commissioned art of Norman Rockwell at the Henry Ford also embodies the wonder and innovation of industrial America. Study the awe in the art of *Harper's Weekly* of the 1800s or the wonder in the artwork of Victorian machinery in the novels of Jules Verne. Look at the architecture in our old industrial cities, which is representative of larger vision. Industry does bring awe and wonder with its problems.

There have been many books of the declines of American industries. Most of these come from a political viewpoint, economic viewpoint, or a social viewpoint. Others in business have looked to place the blame on workers or unions. Many have also attacked the poor quality of management and lack of vision. Some blame the lack of investment of big business. Such perspectives hide the true complex history and nature; and if we don't understand the complexity, we cannot correct things. It is that history where one must start. While Liberal Arts scholars often point to their mastery in reading *War and Peace,* I claim mastery in reading Adam Smith's 200-year-old, 900-page monster, *Wealth of Nations.* It is in this economic classic where the seeds of de-industrialization are found.

The renaissance of American manufacturing, like America herself, will require political, economic, and social compromise. The answers are not with any one political party or economic group. The answer has parts in both the liberal and conservative views. It will require an "American" viewpoint first espoused by Alexander Hamilton and later by Henry Clay (it will also require Clay's skills in compromising). Today we have become entrenched in party, ideological views, and economic theory which limit our ability to solve the problem. The only political party that had most of the answers — the Whig Party — has been dead for over 160 years. And that party's success was in its single focus on the American economic growth, excluding all social issues in its platform. It is not likely such a party would rise again on the American political scene. Still, I consider myself to be a Whig.

But this is not a story of politics; it a story of workers, managers, and communities. There is no single villain but there are many. The failure to understand how important manufacturing is to a nation is widely shared. I started my career as a steel manager near the seven-mile-long steel mill of Aliquippa, Pennsylvania. A friend of mine in the Jaycees had invited me to the grand opening of his ophthalmology office. As the wine flowed and salmon mousse disappeared, the conversation turned to his two German cars and those overpaid steelworkers. He failed to link his success to the medical benefits enjoyed by those steel workers. Six years later the bankruptcy of that Aliquippa mill led to his own bankruptcy. As it was, another friend had started a lawn service business for those overpaid steelworkers. Whenever a large steel mill or factory closes, it is a loss to the middle class and community as much as the factory workers themselves. The death of American industry is a story of the death of American communities. That death has taken tax money away from our schools and taken markets from our small businesses. The source of this death can be found not in our country, but in the Alps of Switzerland.

CHAPTER 1. THE PRELUDE — THE MONT PÈLERIN SOCIETY

The roots of American de-industrialization go back to April of 1947 in Switzerland. The exact location was Mont Pèlerin, overlooking Lake Geneva. The meeting was assembled by free market economist Friedrich von Hayek at the luxurious Hotel du Parc. Of the 36 free market thinkers present, there were only two reluctant Americans. The most famous was Milton Friedman. Interestingly, much of the funding for the symposium came from American free-market and libertarian groups. The group was committed to promoting the belief that economics was the key to world peace. The majority of participants were Austrian economists interested in starting an international counter-revolution on the level of that of Karl Marx. One plank of their six guiding principles was the "creation of an international order conducive to the safeguarding of peace and liberty and permitting the establishment of harmonious international economic relations."[1] The Society, in particular, opposed government interference and import tariffs, following the ideas of Adam Smith. They also opposed trade unionism, socialism, communism, and even nationalism. They opposed all that seemed wrong with the world. Few at the time realized that the meeting would change industrial America forever. In fact, serious American economists of the time gave it little notice. Most saw the vision of Mont Pèlerin as impractical, utopian, and idealistic.

Many at the conference were philosophers and social scientists more interested in social economics. The Mont Pèlerin economists broke with

1 Mont Pelerin Society, "Statement of Aims," April 6, 1947

tradition. Since Adam Smith in the 1700s, economists had studied social behavior to develop economic theory. The Mont Pèlerin economists were activists looking at economics as a way to change social behavior. They would discuss for hours the reasons for the growth of National Socialism in Germany. While they lamented the rise of communism after World War II, they feared more the rise of a German type national socialism. They saw nationalism in any form as a challenge to world peace. They believed that international unity and world governance were needed to assure peace. They believed free market economics was the foundation of international peace. It would even spread the wealth to the poorer countries. Their views seemed harmless enough at the time and considered less achievable than those one hundred years earlier of Karl Marx.

The premier American economist of the time, John Kenneth Galbraith, was said to have made the following dismissal: "The small remaining band of free market economists met on an Alpine peak to form a society, which, however, soon foundered over a division within its ranks on the question of whether the British Navy should be owned by the government or leased from the private sector."[1] Galbraith couldn't have been more mistaken. By 1974, free market economics would dominate the Western world, and founder Friedrich Hayek would win the 1974 Nobel Prize. The reluctant American attendee, Milton Friedman, became the president of the Mont Pèlerin Society in 1972 and won the Nobel Peace Prize in 1976. By then, Mont Pèlerin economists were taking chairs at the country's more prestigious universities. The Mont Pèlerin Society would have their annual meeting at St. Andrews, Scotland, honoring the bicentennial of Adam Smith's *Wealth of Nations*. The Society that had once been a radical group of economists was mainstream by 1976. Mont Pèlerin economists were now writing the textbooks and being asked to advise presidents. Free market economics became natural law in university classes. The year 1976 would also usher in the Age of American De-industrialization.

While the Mont Pèlerin social economists were meeting in 1947, their opposition was giving them an unintended boost. Traditional Keynesian economists were looking at ways to eliminate world wars also. They, too, believed more trade was a solution. The General Agreement on Tariffs and Trade (GATT) was implemented by the Western nations after World War II to regulate trade and assure the world economic recovery, but the need for GATT was rooted in the Great Depression. World

---

1   William F. Buckley Jr., *Let Us Talk of many Things: The Collected Speeches*, (Basic Books: New York, 2006), p. 224

economists believed the Great Depression had led to two problems: (1) the shutdown of trade, which crippled countries such as England and the United States; and (2) the rise of fascism in Germany and Italy. The Keynesian economists came to the same conclusion as the Mont Pèlerin conference — that trade restrictions were the root cause.

GATT, like the United Nations, has only grown in power with the economic power of the Mont Pèlerin views. The impact of GATT remains in force today, since it established the US dollar as the international currency and America as the leader in free trade. GATT also established the institutions of the World Bank and the International Monetary Fund. GATT would govern international trade from 1947 until 1995, when the World Trade Organization (WTO) replaced it formally. GATT's guiding principles, however, remain in effect today.

No one in 1947 would have envisioned the future scale of American de-industrialization. The year was highlighted by the consumer demand outstripping supply. America was looking at ways to increase imports to help meet demand. Population rankings of the cities were mainly linked to the industrial powerhouses. Detroit was #5, followed by Pittsburgh (#7), St. Louis (#8), Cleveland (#9), Buffalo (#14), and Cincinnati (#18). These cities had been built on over 100 years of American protectionism. Then the Western nations formed the International Monetary Fund (IMF) to help spread trade around the world. Decades later, the IMF would play a key role in the application of Mont Pèlerin Society trade views.

The radical economic views of the Mont Pèlerin Society in 1947 promised a world free of major wars. The Mont Pèlerin Society promoted trade as a basis for world peace and urged a major change in world outlook. That change would have to go beyond simple economic philosophy. Free trade would require a world unity, and the United Nations would be part of that vision. World overview organizations would have to be formed to monitor trade disagreements. Banks would have to link up internationally and offer funds to emerging countries. Nationalism and exceptionalism in countries like America and Germany would have to be tamped down. The Mont Pèlerin Society needed cooperation between nations on a scale that had never been seen. The Western nations would have to spread capital to developing countries, trading wealth and jobs for the promise of peace. Central banks in the West would have to coordinate their monetary policies.

Many might see Mont Pèlerin as a conspiracy, but their stated intentions seemed to concern avoiding another world war. They blamed economic competition as the root of world wars. But enabling worldwide free trade would require the world to function as a single entity to a greater degree than previously seen. Interestingly, the Mont Pèlerin Society was fiercely anti-communist, but its plan was in some ways a type of world socialism that would remove economic differences between nations. No wonder mainstream economists of the time saw their plan as highly unlikely to succeed. Yet the Mont Pèlerin Society's anti-communist stand was one of the reasons it was initially adopted by the West: as a strategy to stop the growth of communism.

Friedrich von Hayek had warned the first attendees of the Mont Pèlerin Society that the counterrevolution would take decades; and this one would alter the government not by a movement from the streets but from the halls of academia. The battle, or conversion, would first have to come at the world's greatest universities. The base for the new views of the Mont Pèlerin Society had evolved out of the economics department at the University of Vienna in Austria and had found followers in British universities.

The root of the Mont Pèlerin evolution in Vienna started with Carl Menger (1840–1921), who hoped to make Adam Smith's theory of capitalism more compassionate. Menger also wanted to address the many criticisms of capitalism being made by the increasingly popular vision of socialism. Menger died in 1921, but his views continued to evolve with the torch being passed to Ludwig von Mises (1881–1973) at the University of Vienna. Mises's ideas of world harmony through economics were not popular with the Nazi Party of Germany, forcing him to become an exiled professor at New York University. Mises's ideas were no more popular with mainstream American economists; however, he was free to write and lecture on his views. Mises seemed to be a harmless academic, writing papers opposing socialism and capitalism's use of Keynesian economics as well, which he saw as not much different from the central planning of communist countries. Mises made some incremental progress on economic thought in the United States.

Mises's greatest student at Vienna was Friedrich A. Hayek (1899–1992). Hayek would take the first steps to popularize this new version of free trade economics. Hayek took his economics to the streets. Hayek published a condensed version of his book, *The Road to Serfdom*, in *Readers' Digest* in 1945. The book played on America's fascination with freedom and its fear of communism. Hayek would also be exiled by the Nazis and went to Kings College, Cambridge, where he would argue directly with the greatest economist of the time, Maynard Keynes. They would often debate while on air raid patrol of the roof of the college during the war. After the war, Hayek would join the great American economist, Milton Friedman, at the University of Chicago.

It would be Milton Friedman, who had reluctantly attended the Mont Pèlerin Conference, who would change America's philosophy. Friedman had shifted his thinking before. He had gone from being a socialist in the 1930s to Keynesian New Dealer by the end of the decade. He believed in government intervention to control the economy. In 1950, when Friedrich von Hayek joined him at the University of Chicago, the new economic philosophy started to take roots. After years of study at the University of Chicago, Friedman slowly converted to the free trade and international capitalism of the Mont Pèlerin Society. The University of Chicago became the center of Mont Pèlerinism in the United States.

As American economists moved towards the Mont Pèlerin philosophy, so did American politicians in both parties. It would be a revolutionary shift in thinking and philosophy that took place at American universities with no real public debate. This would be a silent reversal of labor and manufacturing approaches. Peace had priority over economic prosperity. After the war Washington started to prepare the nation for free trade as a means to assure world peace. The Kennedy Administration was first to embrace the use of trade as a peace strategy. However, John F. Kennedy realized that free trade, as envisioned by the Mont Pèlerin Society, would cost a lot of American jobs. The Kennedy Administration passed the Trade Adjustment Assistance Act in 1962 as part of a total free trade package. The bill got little press in a nation that had few imports other than nickel-and-dime toys; while in 1962, prosperity and lack of imports made free trade of little interest to American workers. Free trade at the time was understood to boost the exports that poured out of America in an embarrassment of riches. Even the unions in 1962 supported free trade because international commerce was a big source of American jobs.

The Trade Adjustment Assistance Act in 1962 called for payments to be made as additions to unemployment compensation. It wasn't until 1974 that any real need surfaced for the Act. Then the program was expanded under the Trade Act of 1974. The program never covered the losses to workers or their communities. Kennedy's words in 1962 would ring true but hollow: "When considerations of national policy make it desirable to avoid higher tariffs, those injured by that competition should not be required to bear the full brunt of the impact. Rather, the burden of economic adjustment should be borne in part by the Federal Government."[1]

Kennedy, like many of his predecessors, seemed more concerned with what to do about displaced workers than how to keep American industry strong against the foreign competition. In fact, the Kennedy and Johnson Administration policies would send a strong message to American steel that it was going to shrink to allow for world trade. The common myth was that steel didn't invest in new technology, but the facts are far different. Even though return on revenues only averaged five percent in the 1960s, the industry invested $2 billion a year in technology.[2] After making investments, President Kennedy would refuse to allow steel companies to raise prices to recoup their investments. The political environment crushed steel stocks in the 1960s, making those companies seek to diversify into non steel areas. It also left steel companies, with depressed stock prices, vulnerable to takeover by conglomerates. By the end of the decade, 12 steel companies were taken over, including big names such as Jones & Laughlin, Youngstown Sheet & Tube, Crucible Steel, and Jessop Steel. The US government had opened the steel industry to decline by interfering with the free market domestically. The results of Mont Pèlerin were now being seen.

In the first decades after World War II, the slow implementation of the Mont Pèlerin plan and Hayek economics had little impact on America. Initially, war-worn Europe and Japan offered no serious manufacturing challenges, so free trade and the high dollar hurt manufacturing exports. As American factories started to age, Europe and Japan were building modernized plants. America even helped with the rebuilding. The Keynesian approach seemed secure in the 1960s, but things were changing under the radar. In 1965, Maynard Keynes was *Time Magazine's* Man of the Year, when his economic theory reached its peak at American universities and political circles. The call for free trade was on the rise as a means to attack communism. The real change came in the 1960s with the full implementation of free trade economics and the conversion of our political parties. That conversion was not based on the merits of the economic theory but on the promise of stopping the growth of communism — any nation that wanted to be part of the profitable trade with the West could not go over to the communist side. These promises allowed

1 Papers of John F. Kennedy 1963, *Public Papers of the Presidents of the United States,*(Washington: Government Printing Office)

2 William T. Hogan, *The 1970s: Critical Years for Steel,* (Lexington: Lexington Books, 1972), p. 17

Hayek's economics to win over the Republican Party which had been the protector of US industry for 100 years.

Friedman flipped the conservative Republican view of scientific protectionism and national capitalism. The hook was not trade but Hayek's and the Mont Pèlerin Society's notion of little government intervention. It reversed the New Deal movement, which to Hayek was reminiscent of communism. Hayek's approach called for freedom from government, domestically and internationally. Unfortunately, his views on free trade came with the package. The ideas of small government attracted Friedman to Barry Goldwater, Richard Nixon, and later Ronald Reagan. Reagan applied the small government approach with success but he was always uncomfortable with the now apparent trend that free trade seemed to be destroying American jobs. Still, American industrial dominance seemed strong enough to take on other manufacturing countries of the time. Then the new world industrial order began to change radically. Reagan also realized that "Reagan Democrats" backed him on small government and overregulation but didn't understand the free trade ideas of the overall philosophy. In addition, Margaret Thatcher in England embraced the philosophy of Mont Pèlerin. What was clear to most people was simply the idea that Hayek's economic theory would unite the West through free trade and strengthen it vis-à-vis the Communist bloc.

By the time Bill Clinton regained the White House for the Democrats, all the preeminent economic advisors were followers of Mont Pèlerin. NAFTA was a free-trade bill that would bring cheap labor competition across our Mexican border. So Democrats slowly adopted free trade while trying to balance it against union resistance. Clinton, like Reagan, remained uncomfortable with free trade, but economists sold the Mont Pèlerin view as a total package. By the 1990s, there was hardly a critical voice for the politicians to turn to in America's major universities. The Clinton, Bush, and Obama years considered trade problems as an industry problem. Tariffs were sometimes temporarily given to an industry, but the real problem in overall economic policy was ignored.

The result of America's embracing of the free trade approach today has been widespread de-industrialization. It has not brought the peace that it promised, and a worldwide shortage of energy has replaced earlier reasons for war. Imports have been flooding America for decades and our major export has been our wealth. This balancing of global wealth has not helped the world's poor. It only destroyed the evolution of good paying jobs in America, spreading low paying jobs around the world. American producers are now forced to compete with the cost of goods made in sweat shops, to keep labor costs as low as they are in Third World countries. Major American companies have adapted far better than labor, by becoming transnational.

On the whole, workers around the world are worse off. The shift in policy has destroyed the American middle class. We have lost the war of words. Tariff-free trade has been labeled as necessary for capitalism and democracy, and fair trade is a term only used by anti-American trouble makers. Yet capitalism and even democracy were rooted in fair and even protective trade practices.

The real argument between free trade and protectionism in America is much older than the theories of Hayek and Keynes, going back to Alexander Hamilton and our first administration. When the American Revolution began in 1776, that was the year that Adam Smith published his 900-page, two-pound manifesto of free trade. It is the *War and Peace* of non-fiction. And even today, the least read, second most published, and most often misquoted book remains Adam Smith's *Wealth of Nations*. It is rarely, truly misquoted, since the few writers who do quote it have had to punish themselves by reading it, including its 25-page discussion on the archaic Corn Laws of England — in Old English. The 1776 world reflected in *Wealth of Nations* has remained a model for today's world but it was based on a reality far different from today's. It is used to justify the call for free trade, but in 1776 the English-speaking world was yet to enter the Industrial Revolution. World trade was centered on agricultural products. The trade of Adam Smith's day was corn, wheat, furs, spices, ginseng, tobacco, and cotton. Adam Smith was a true genius in understanding the aggregate operation of world economics in a pre-industrial world, but his analogies of local craftsman represented his world view of manufacturing. Adam Smith's world had no steam engines, deep coal mines, machine shops, automated machines, and only a handful of factories. But despite the gaps, Smith's concept of free trade would sweep the world's economic philosophies and England would be first.

Free trade would eventually de-industrialize England in the late 1890s. The decline of England's once great industrial might was obvious to its citizens, but the politicians, the Treasury, and the bankers maintained that more free trade was the way to return to greatness. Still, it was haunting that America, a once backward country of farmers, had overtaken England in industrial output. America had risen in the 1890s to an industrial giant. The great economist of the early 1900s, John Maynard Keynes, lamented the fall of the British as the nation entered the twentieth century. Britain had already morphed from the leader of the

Industrial Revolution into an international banking center; and banking employed few in comparison to manufacturing. It was the scientific protectionism and trade reciprocity of President William McKinley that took America to first place as the dominant industrial nation. Keynes came to believe that the heart of a nation is in its manufacturing, and Britain's heart had stopped beating. Seeing the economic destruction of his nation, Keynes reconsidered the free trading ideas of Adam Smith and changed to a balanced view of trade where tariffs might be necessary.[1]

The powerful surge of American manufacturing through a blend of scientific protectionism and national capitalism impressed Bismarck of Germany. Germany would study and adopt the McKinley approach. Germany protected its iron and steel industry, making it a rival of the United States. Like America, Germany rose to an industrial super power.

Years later, Keynes would argue that the Versailles Peace Treaty after World War I would lead to political upheaval in Germany. The treaty cut the manufacturing heart out of Germany. The treaty clearly punished Germany economically by taking away its coal mines in Alsace-Lorraine and restricting the use of the Rhine River to feed the German industrial heartland. Keynes believed that if a nation's ability to manufacture things was destroyed, then social unrest would follow. Keynes was proved right, as Germany could not afford to allow its industry to be chained and a proud people revolted at the enforce impoverishment. Keynes's views, however, were readily accepted in the New Deal politicians of America. Economic guru John Kenneth Galbraith carried the Keynesian torch from the 1930s to the 1950s. The Keynesian approach of government-driven economics became the world's guiding economic theory.

Keynes preferred free trade but found it hard to impose it as national policy. Keynes argued that there would be times that a nation would require tariffs, which he called "iron rations."[2] He correctly foresaw the rise of National Socialism in Germany. Keynes's view would be opposed by economist Friedrich von Hayek, not over Germany's need for manufacturing, but how to achieve it. They had plenty of time to debate their views as they were on night watch for possible German air attack of their employer, King's College, Cambridge, in the early 1940s. Keynes saw a role for tariffs as an economics of government; Hayek believed in free international trade without government intervention.

---

1 Nicholas, Wapshott, *Keynes Hayek: The Clash That Defined Modern Economics*, (New York: W. W. Norton & Company, 2011), p. 62

2 Ibid., p. 61

The senior economist Maynard Keynes would be discredited some-what by the Great Depression and the war. Yet Keynesian economists dominated the universities in the 1940s, so even the theory's failures would not soon result in a new approach. However, Hayek was the rising star of anti-Keynesian economics, with the idea of free trade as a tool for world peace and a defense against Marxism and socialism. Mont Pèlerin free trade would soon become dominant in all the various "schools" of economics.

This view would come to dominate economic thought and the policy of the Western nations. It would come to take America down the same path of the British Empire with the economics of Adam Smith. It would find international banking support in those Western nations because banking profited most by international trade.

While Hayek's view opposed socialism as a "false god," his economics would become in itself a type of international socialism re-distributing the wealth of nations.[1] What both could agree on was that economics was a tool for social reform. They would see economics elevated to a social science and a curriculum of its own, separate from that of business colleges.

In the 1970s, Hayek and the Mont Pèlerin Society were shocked to see their views take root in the Western world. Princeton's Nobel laureate economist, Alan Blinder, declared: "By about 1980, it was hard to find an American macroeconomist under the age of forty who professed to be a Keynesian."[2] At major universities the only group that would sit at the lunch table with the Keynesians was visiting creationists. It was not, however, the free trade views of Hayek that had brought the conversion so much as the general idea of low taxes and little government. In fact, it was some of America's strongest nationalists such as Ronald Reagan who let the devil in the back door with the reduction of government in general. What they had not seen clearly was that Hayek's trade ideas would result in a decline in American business. As presidents had only Hayek-style advisors to choose from by 1990, even presidents such as Bill Clinton adopted the trade views. In fairness, both Reagan and Clinton were disturbed by the impact on American manufacturing.

The problem reflected the polarization of America itself — no middle ground — you were either a Hayekian or a Keynesian. Fearing to compro-

---

1 F. A. Hayek, *The Road to Serfdom: The Definitive Edition*, (Chicago: University of Chicago Press, 2007), p. 223

2 Alan S. Blinder, "The Fall and Rise of Keynesian Economics," *Economic Record*, December 1988

mise on any part of the philosophy because it might weaken the overall argument, policymakers felt they had few options. The economic polarization split the conservatives who, for almost a century, had maintained national tariffs. It would seem inconsistent to allow government intervention in tariffs while asking for more de-regulation, with less taxes and spending. Furthermore, the Hayekian approach, while denouncing government intervention, had no problem with Federal Reserve intervention. Only libertarians seemed to question the power of the Federal Reserve. This lack of compromise and clear vision meant the political tools remained frozen as de-industrialization took down a manufacturing nation. To the average citizen lacking a degree in economics, what was happening was beyond comprehension. The citizen, therefore, defaulted to the opinion of his or her political party, which was probably just as confused.

It may seem strange to some that a winning economic idea coming out of academia could change the world, but remember, these are the men behind government policies. They are the court advisors in our halls of government. One of the world's most famous economists, John M. Keynes, said it best: "the ideas of economists and political philosophers, both when they are right and when they are wrong, are more powerful than commonly understood. Indeed the world is ruled by little else. Practical men, who believe they are exempt from any intellectual influences, are usually the slaves of some defunct economist. Madmen in authority, who hear voices in the air, are distilling their frenzy from some academic scribbler of a few years back."[1] This may be the best explanation of American de-industrialization. Still, it defies reason that countries like Britain and America would so readily give up their industrial might and wealth.

How did the free trade economics of Adam Smith, who never saw the Industrial Revolution or even the steam engine, capture the minds of the leaders of the world's greatest industrial nations? At least for America and for England, who embraced the free trade philosophy in the 1800s, it was based on growing their nations as banking centers and shipping nations. As early as the great J.P. Morgan, American bankers favored free trade economics against the industrialists of the period. Morgan realized that for the big banks, profitability was a matter of volume, not which way the products moved. Like a casino, the issue became increasing trade volume. Furthermore, international trade opened up new global opportunities in profitability for banks. Big banks have become transnational

---

1 Friedrich Hayek, *The Road to Serfdom: The Definitive Edition*, (Chicago: University of Chicago Press, 2007), p. 32

with little roots to their home countries; thus, they are by nature "free traders." But the Hayekian approach offered something far more attractive to bankers in its monetary policy, which allowed the banks, not government, to have a larger role in economic policy.

But how did free trade win over the average American citizen who still believed America to be exceptional? They were accustomed to thinking of a kind of national capitalism, with barriers to limit foreign competition. Again, the battle of language was fought and won at America's universities by the free traders. The trick was to make "free trade" synonymous with democracy and capitalism. The term "fair trade" was overtaken by the older term — protectionism. Protectionism had been the cornerstone of conservatives for decades. It required Republican protectionism of 100 years to be overlooked, not discredited. In effect, these Mont Pèlerin supporters had to decouple nationalism and protection. Hayek's famous book, *The Road to Serfdom*, had won over hardcore conservatives such as Barry Goldwater with its call for limited government; but conservatives were nationalistic by nature. That difficult bridge was crossed during a meeting of the Mont Pèlerin Society at Hillsdale College in Michigan in 1975, where the now popular Milton Friedman sealed the deal. Friedman used the meeting to tie political science, economic history, and political history into economics.[1] Conservatives were hooked by making free trade a necessary component to the idea of capitalism, marketplace freedom, and limited government. Free trade became the philosophical heart of the American democracy, ignoring 150 years of history.

Similar Mont Pèlerin Society meetings in England would win over Margaret Thatcher; and in 1976 as she took over as Prime Minster, Friedman and Hayek would be regular visitors to 10 Downing Street. Now as Hayek had predicted at Mont Pèlerin, "after roaming in the wilderness for thirty years, Hayekians had overcome Keynes' influence."[2] While the Hayekian view of limited government and lower taxes proved convenient for conservatives, its lesser economic planks such as free trade would undermine the industries of the Western nations. The problem of trade and de-industrialization fell between the great divide of the two political parties in America.

The results of free trade have been the same for centuries — that is, a decline of industrialization and manufacturing. Liberals who had tradi-

---

1 Nicholas Wapshott, *Keynes Hayek: The Clash That Defined Modern Economics*, (New York: W. W. Norton & Company, 2011), p. 250
2 Nicholas Wapshott, *Keynes Hayek: The Clash That Defined Modern Economics*, (New York: W. W. Norton & Company, 2011), p. 269

tionally defended free trade for the farmers were now forced to be defend-
ers of protectionism by default. In effect, free trade would see only a limited debate in America. Industry might find some limited support from
the Democrats and their union members who appreciated protectionism,
or limited protection from Republicans based on their nationalist base.
The citizens in the Rust Belt were told, as in Britain of the 1890s, that
free trade was not the problem but the solution. Economic concepts are
not readily understood by the public, who are left susceptible to political
manipulation. Americans accepted the idea that free trade was necessary
for business when for decades imports had overwhelmed exports. The
slow, segmented approach of de-industrialization allowed the cancer to
progress without a widespread national opposition. Political polarization prevented a truly national opposition from forming.

The slow pace of de-industrialization over 60 years has not given us
the sharp, deep crisis needed to force an honest review of the effect of
free trade policies on the United States. The gradual devolution allowed
the public to become numb to the devastation of our cities. Polarization
of views blocked the implementation of practical solutions. This slow
economic cancer does not work like the traditional "business cycle,"
which might run its course in a few years. Even the long and hard Great
Depression, lasting ten years, was followed by several economic expan-
sions. If you compressed the effects of the current de-industrialization
into a ten-year time frame, it would be obvious that the devastation
has far exceeded anything seen by this country. Even the devastation
to Europe's and Japan's industry from World War II lasted only 10 to
15 years before it was completely rebuilt (with international support).
But de-industrialization has relentlessly progressed for 60 years with
no prospect of long-term rebuilding. Who has really benefited from the
Mont Pèlerin economics?

Can free traders claim that Mont Pèlerin has brought peace to the
world? America has been at war almost continuously for decades. Why
then is free trade politically so popular? The Right sells it as the cornerstone of capitalism. The Left uses it as an international political tool. But
we are all supporters in an important sense: Free trade favors the biggest
voter block, that of consumers. It gave us all those low Wal-Mart prices
— while at the same time reducing wages so that one could only shop at
Wal-Mart.

Many economists see (or at least have sold) it as part of our innovative successes or a form of "creative destruction," that ushers in the Information Age. In fact, it would be economist Joseph Schumpeter (1883–

1950), one of the founders of the Austrian school of economics and later a member of the Mont Pèlerin Society, who used the idea of "creative destruction" to put a positive spin on de-industrialization.[1] The story of de-industrialization in America lacks a clear villain, and that might be the secret of its success. De-industrialization attacks and destroys locally and slowly; its widespread effects have remained under the radar for most of the public at any point in time. The closing of a large steel mill or rubber factory is portrayed in the media as a local disaster (or a problem for stockholders) rather than a national crisis. But it progresses city by city, industry by industry, and region by region. Almost everyone has felt the pain; even the federal and state governments are feeling the pain of lack of tax funds from industry.

By 2005, the views espoused in 1947 by the Mont Pèlerin Society were the mainstream stuff of economic textbooks. Employees laid off as a result of de-industrialization now have to face the theory in the classroom as they go back to school in an effort to prepare for new careers. A single mom, Alison Murray, displaced from a Fostoria, Ohio, sparkplug factory, faced this irony on her return to school. Ms. Murray noted in an interview with the editor of *Harper's Magazine*: "So it was like getting slapped in the face... the very first class I took, the very first page of the textbook[2] [justifies my layoff]." The destruction of a town or city or even a country is treated as progress or a shining example of freedom via world capitalism. Ms. Murray would argue with her professor that the theory sounds good until you live its application.

The de-industrialization of a society has a known future. De-industrialization is not new. Britain faced a slow de-industrialization over decades beginning in when Great Britain fully embraced the free trade theories of Adam Smith in the early 1840s; and the crack in the great edifice of British manufacturing was already obvious in 1851. Queen Victoria and her husband Prince Albert started planning for the world's greatest fair in the 1840s. It was initiated as a celebration of British technology and industry, but it would not follow the plan. Known as the Great Exhibition, by the time the event got off the ground in 1851, a backward, protectionist country stunned many of the industrial equipment exhibitors by winning most of the prizes. The fledgling America's great showing might be likened to having Korea win in overall gold medals in the

---

1   Mark Skousen, *Vienna & Chicago: Friends or Foes?*, (Washington: Capital Press, 2006), p. 40
2   John MacArthur, "The Deindustrialization of America," *Counterpunch*, August 5, 2011, p. 6

today's Olympics. With its advanced machines and tools, America was already a manufacturing power on equal with England. Prince Albert was so shocked he formed a committee to detail how America had surged ahead of industrial Britain. The list of conclusions is informative:

(1) A logic to exploit their abundance of energy and natural resources.

(2) A high literacy rate. America was behind only Scotland in 1851.

(3) Few barriers to organizing business (such as individual taxes, regulatory rules, industry taxes, and fees).

(4) Workers' lack of resistance to innovation. In England, workers were protected (that is to say, businesses were hampered) by strong labor unions. What's more, radical laborers stood firmly in the way of mechanization, modernization that would reduce the number of jobs. In the early part of the century, a group of working men known as the Ludderites hid in Sherwood Forest by day and burned automated factory equipment by night.

(5) Use of high tariffs to protect its major industries.

(6) A highly competitive nature.

Interestingly, today these can be considered America's weaknesses and maybe China's strengths. In fact, when these characteristics and conclusions are proposed to students today, they believe it's about China in 2012. Britain had started the move to free trade in the 1840s, and Britain's history has become America's reality and future.

Britain also made a conscious decision to de-industrialize based on the idea that the country would become a world trading empire and world financial center. Their native son Adam Smith's ideas of free trade made sense and supported their world trade view. Factories closed and wages started to decline as early as 1840 as Britain moved to a free trade approach. The American economic nationalism was creating a new world power by 1850. By the 1860s, British machine makers and tool and die makers were emigrating from Britain to America. By the 1870s, an even more protectionist America was leading in machine and railroad equipment manufacture. Britain remained a proud apostle of free trade. In the 1890s, protectionist America eclipsed Britain's iron, steel, machine, glass, ceramic, chemical, and most other industries. Otto von Bismarck, founder and first chancellor (1871–1890) of the German Empire, saw the decline of Britain and directed German industry to follow the American path, using focused protectionist principles. Britain's decline in manufacturing was accompanied by its decline as the world's superpower. America and Germany would rise, with their programmatic protectionism allowing them strong economic growth.

Chapter 2. America's Different Path

The period of 1776 through the 1920s brought an American industrialization to world dominance. The reason for that climb to dominance was a clear government policy to industrialize the nation, going back to the 1790s. The father of American manufacturing is none other than Federalist Alexander Hamilton. Hamilton's 1794 *Report on Manufactures* should be a guiding document. The following is an important excerpt: "But though it were true, that the immediate and certain effect of regulations controlling the competition of foreign with domestic fabrics was an increase of price, it is universally true, that the contrary is the ultimate effect with every successful manufacture. When a domestic manufacture has attained to perfection, and has engaged in the prosecution of it a competent number of Persons, it invariably becomes cheaper. Being free from the heavy charges which attend the importation of foreign commodities, it can be afforded, and accordingly seldom ever fails to be sold, cheaper, in process of time, than was the foreign article for which it is a substitute. The internal competition which takes place, soon does away everything like monopoly, and by degrees reduces the price of the article to the minimum of a reasonable profit on the capital employed. This accords with the reason of the thing and with experience. Whence it follows, that it is in the interest of a community, with a view to eventual and permanent economy, to encourage the growth of manufactures, in a national view, a temporary enhancement of price must always be well compensated by a permanent reduction of it."[1] Hamilton's thesis would be proven in the 1800s.

Tariffs allowed domestic manufacture to be built and they encouraged technology investment that actually lowered prices in the long run. In addition, domestic competition was strong enough to prevent monopolistic behavior. Hamilton saw capitalism as national in scope and civic in nature. Like the Mont Pèlerin Society, Hamilton saw economics as a means to achieve a goal. Hamilton's and the Federalist views led directly to the "American System" of Henry Clay. The "American System" was national capitalism. Clay became a champion of industry to New England, Ohio, Pennsylvania, and Kentucky.

American industrialization was directly related to the political foundation of Henry Clay's "American System." This system was a protectionist approach to protect industries via tariffs, and an aggressive approach to national improvements such as roads and canals. It put the American economy ahead of economic theory, using government intervention, if necessary, to advance growth. The Federalists and the Jeffersonians would split on this issue to form the Whig Party.

To fully grasp the roots of Clay's economic philosophy, one must first understand Thomas Jefferson's vision of the nation. Jefferson envisioned an agrarian society of farmers and merchants. In 1790, an estimated 90 percent of the American population was employed in agriculture. His vision demanded free trade to assure that crops could move into foreign markets readily. Jefferson had grown up in a tobacco and cotton culture that depended on European purchases of their crops. While he believed in farm self-sufficiency, he feared the industrialization that he had seen in Europe.

Hamilton, on the other hand, saw America's freedom rooted in its ability to achieve economic freedom through manufacturing and banking. Hamilton the soldier was well aware of the role of technology and manufacturing in the ability of a nation to win wars. He believed that manufacturing was fundamental to America's freedom. As a young officer, Hamilton found the colonial army constrained by lack of iron cannon and rifles because of the lack of American manufacture. America moved quickly to develop iron making, which had been forbidden under colonial law (to protect the British iron industry). America first picked up cheap dumped British iron after the Revolutionary War, only to be caught again short of manufactured arms for the War of 1812. Interest-

---

1 Alexander Hamilton, *Report on Manufactures*, January 15, 1790

ingly, President William McKinley would have the same experience in his regiment during the Civil War, and later it was his term as US President that was the golden era for protectionism.

Hamilton, however, in his time, had remained as opposed to across-the-board import duties. Like many of his federalist friends, he believed that financial systems were the basis for industrialization. Still, at the very root of Hamiltonian Federalism was government's role to promote industry. Actually, the Federalists were split on tariffs, some seeing no need for them because America lacked manufacturing anyway, and others seeing tariffs as a source of federal revenue. The Federalist papers remain mostly silent on tariffs; however, Hamilton envisioned protectionist tariffs to help particular industries develop. Hamilton specially suggested: "protective tariffs or prohibiting the exportation of competing manufactures until American producers in a given industry were firmly established; prohibiting the exportation of raw materials; granting bounties and other direct subsides; awarding premiums or prizes 'to reward some particular excellence or superiority, some extraordinary exertion or skill'; exempting imported raw materials from duties and granting drawbacks of such duties; encouraging invention; inspecting manufactured products; and facilitating internal commerce through an extension of the banking system and improvement of transportation facilities."[1] Tariffs on non-agricultural products were new in the 1790s. Britain, by contract, protected its industry by colonial acts of Parliament.

Both Jefferson and Hamilton were constrained by the agricultural nature and lack of manufacturing in America at the time. However, earlier British prohibitions such as the British Iron Act of 1750 had infuriated Scotch-Irish iron makers like James McKinley (William McKinley's grandfather) in Western Pennsylvania. In particular, the Scotch-Irish moved to the Ohio frontier to avoid tax laws. The Iron Act of 1750 allowed for all raw bars of smelted iron (known as pig iron) to be shipped to England duty-free but outlawed the colonial production of iron products such as kettles, skillets, stoves, forged iron for guns, and steel for the blacksmith shop. These frontiersmen remembered and vowed never to be economically restrained again by any government — British or American. Many of these same Scotch-Irish would flee Western Pennsylvania to Ohio, Kentucky, and Tennessee to avoid the federal tax on whiskey (their primary marketable good) in 1794 and would become part of the political base of frontier politician Henry Clay. His political base often

---

1 Forrest McDonald, *Alexander Hamilton*, (New York: W.W. Norton, 1982), p. 236

disagreed with Clay — they wanted cheap imported goods but, like Clay, believed in America.

The rural nature of early America colors the approach taken in the Federalists papers. But make no mistake about it; if the Federalists were to see the erosion of the manufacturing base today, they would be appalled. The Federalists believed firmly in the function of government to regulate commerce, expand banking to support business, and build infrastructure. The Federalists were supporters of tariffs to protect American agriculture but foresaw a day when a different movement would be necessary to promote manufacturing. James Madison also argued the regulation of foreign commerce was a function of the federal government.[1] They would quickly see through the idea of "free" trade and realize the nature of the economic warfare in which we find ourselves. They would well remember their dependence on England for iron when the War of 1812 began. That lesson would help form the Whig party that saw manufacturing as fundamental to national security. The Whig Party saw strong manufacturing as part of national defense, and even Adam Smith saw national defense trumping free trade concepts. The anti-government Scotch-Irish, who rebelled against federal taxes, believed that the federal government should promote manufacturing as a national defense issue. These patriots saw that economic freedom was necessary for political freedom. They had suffered for centuries both in Europe and America from British control of their manufacturing. Indeed, the American declaration of economic freedom preceded the Declaration of Independence by two years.

The needs of innovative frontier manufacturers would promote the idea of protective tariffs. At the time, Western Pennsylvania was the heart of iron manufacture, and it was here that the move from Jeffersonian free trade to Henry Clay's American System first strengthened. Pennsylvania Congressman Henry Baldwin supported Henry Clay's American System with an iron fist in the early 1800s. Pennsylvania Senator Judge Wilkins became known as the "iron knight" in his support of iron tariffs. The manufacturers ultimately wrestled the vote away from the Jefferson Democrats as Andrew Jackson's policies turned anti-manufacturing. These manufacturers often held dinners for national protectionists such as Mathew Carey and Henry Clay. Nearby manufacturing cities such as Steubenville, Ohio, and Wheeling, Virginia, developed a manufacturing network through Clay and Carey. Matthew Carey would

---

1 Federalist Papers, James Madison No. 41 and No. 42

become a proponent of managed trade and an advisor to a young Whig, Abraham Lincoln. Clay and Carey (and Hamilton) would be heroes to future presidents Lincoln and McKinley. This area of "transylvania" (West Pennsylvania, Ohio, Kentucky, and West Virginia) with its old Whig roots would win the presidencies for both Lincoln and McKinley. They would carry the torch of Henry Clay and the Whig Party.

Henry Clay was a Virginian lawyer who moved to Kentucky to launch his career. In 1810, he was elected to the United States Congress. Clay was a nationalist, patriot, republican, Founder of the Whig Party, and a Federalist. In his junior years in the Senate, he advocated a strong national bank and a national road and canal system. Often Clay favored the good of the nation over his own constituents in Kentucky. His oratory, skills in arriving at a compromise, and patriotism brought him quickly to the position of Speaker of the House. Clay not only fashioned the position of House Speaker, but he formed the powerful standing committees (such as the Ways and Means Committee, which would be the pedestal from which William McKinley launched his career years later). Clay also created a Congressional Committee on Manufactures to help stimulate \ manufacturing as Alexander Hamilton had suggested years earlier. Clay appointed members for these powerful committees and thus, centralized legislative power under the position of Speaker. Clay used the power to create a national infrastructure for an industrial America. Clay's vision of an industrial empire took him from Jeffersonian Republicanism to Federalism and then to conservatism and republicanism. Some Federalists, however, were New England-based free traders because of the shipping industry. Clay's arguments and the rise of American manufacturing won over many New England Federalists who believed in the destiny of the republic of the United States as a world power. Clay had grown up in the economic debates between the Jeffersonian and the Federalists and would make his support of manufacturing into a national movement and eventually a political party.

The War of 1812 and the economic warfare that followed extended into the 1820s, proving Hamilton's view on the need for economic independence. The British attempted to destroy the evolving US textile industry by dumping huge quantities of British textiles on American docks. The British similarly cut prices and sold cheap pig iron to suppress the growing American pig iron industry. Henry Brougham in Parliament declared, "It was well worthwhile to incur a loss upon the first exportation, in order, by the glut, to stifle in the cradle, those rising manufactures in the United States."[1] The British were more successful in this type of war than those fought with gunpowder, bankrupting hundreds of American manufacturers and closing charcoal iron furnaces throughout the country. The Northeast put political pressure on Congress to save its textile-manufacturing base, and the Pennsylvania, Virginia, and Ohio pig iron producers and users joined the political pressure. That pressure would build and lead to the formation of the "American System" of Henry Clay.

Congress hesitated to put in place protective iron tariffs, torn by competing regional goals. The Southern cotton growers opposed any tariffs on British goods, believing Britain would retaliate with tariffs on cotton and tobacco. The major portion of the South's cotton and tobacco went to Great Britain for processing. Furthermore, even the Northeast representatives were torn between the textile mills and the merchants who lived by shipping goods abroad through free trade. The struggle in Congress in 1816 would produce a new champion in Henry Clay, Speaker of the House of Representatives. The Congress appeared hopelessly deadlocked on the issue. Clay built an alliance for the tariffs based on nationalism versus regional politics. The debate took place in a temporary brick building (at the site of today's Supreme Court), known as the "Old Brick capitol." The city of Washington lay in ruins after being sacked by the British and offered a stark reminder of the need for a strong defense. Clay found allies in Southerners John Calhoun and President James Madison, who would help tip the balance. Clay brought in the middle state representatives who had suffered from British dumping of iron products as well to suppress American industry. He astutely played on rising nationalism and anti-British sentiments to bring in enough Southern votes to pass the tariff. The embryonic Pig Iron Aristocracy rallied behind Henry Clay. The result was America's first tariff — the Tariff of 1816 — which established duties of 25 percent on cotton and wool products and 30 percent on iron products. The Tariff of 1816 would underpin the financial security of the Pennsylvania ironworker families such as that of the future William McKinley.

After the Tariff of 1816, Clay not only broke away completely from Jefferson's thinking but from his own Federalist leanings of free trade. The Federalists were split because tariffs appeared to be a heresy. Many Federalists were free-trader Yankees even though they favored helping national industries. The split would eventually lead to the Whig Party.

---

1 Quentin Skrabec, *The Pig Iron Aristocracy: The Triumph of American Protectionism*, (Westminster: Heritage Books, 2008) p. 44

Clay forged a new path for American capitalism that was nationalistic and economic with his American System. It was a Magna Carta of American economic freedom. Clay realized that economic war was a reality in the world of the 1800s. Clay's vision was similar to Jefferson's, differing only in that industry was substituted for agriculture. Like Eisenhower in the 1950s, Clay envisioned a system of national transportation to support industrial growth. Clay molded a powerful new philosophy which blended Jeffersonian independence with economic manifest destiny. Clay went further to justify his American System by blending in American moral superiority with nationalistic capitalism. The momentum had turned in Clay's favor by 1824. The struggle, however, would not end as skillful opponents such as Daniel Webster arose.

In 1824, Congress moved to debate even more extensive tariffs. Clay, the famed orator, would emerge as leader of this industrial movement. He thundered in Congress with an oratory reminiscent of Patrick Henry a generation earlier:

> "Is there no remedy within the reach of the government? Are we doomed to behold our industry languish and decay yet more and more? But there is a remedy, and the remedy consists in modifying our foreign policy, and adopting a genuine American System. We must naturalize the arts in our country, and we must naturalize them by the only means, which the wisdom of nations has yet discovered to be effectual — by adequate protection against the otherwise overwhelming influence of foreigners. This can only be accomplished by the establishment of a tariff."[1]

Further increasing tariffs faced tough political opposition. Clay struggled against an equally articulate and dynamic speaker, Daniel Webster, and the entire Southern wing of the House of Representatives. Clay had strong support from the "Pig Iron Aristocracy in the person of Henry Baldwin, the "iron knight," from Pittsburgh. In New England, Daniel Webster of New Hampshire opposed the tariff because it might hurt the New England shipping industry. Clay persisted, and on April 16, 1824, the Tariff of 1824 passed by a vote of 107 to 102.

Recognizing the interests of the cotton and tobacco growers in the South, the breakdown over tariffs between the slave-owning versus non-slave states is more understandable. Non-Slave states voted for the tariff: 89 for and 32 against. Slave states voted against the tariff: 70 vs. 18 voting for the tariff. It was from here that tariffs and slavery would become intertwined.

---

1 Robert Remini, *Henry Clay: Statesman of the Union*, (New York: W. W. Norton & Co., 1991), 230

Ohio supported the tariff, not only in the Mahoning Valley but also in more western counties where an infant wool industry was emerging. Pennsylvania and Ohio's Pig Iron Aristocrats added additional support. US President James Monroe signed the bill in May. The Tariff of 1824 extended the general level of protection to 35 percent *ad valorem* (the percentage of value as represented by the invoice). The Tariff applied to cotton, wool, and iron products and also extended to the hemp producers of Clay's Kentucky.

Clay's politics started a change in what would become the future core of the Whig Party (known as Iron Whigs) and future President McKinley's base — the Mahoning Valley of NE Ohio and NW Pennsylvania, Niles and Youngstown, OH; Canton and Pittsburgh, PA; western Virginia, and Ohio's Western Reserve. Not surprisingly, the geographic area is the heart of today's Rust Belt. These old frontier areas had a large Scotch-Irish population who had opposed with guns the whiskey taxes of the Federalists. They tended to be frontier Jeffersonian, but Clay's protection of wool and iron started to build the base for a new type of Federalist, which no longer had a national party. Industrialization was changing the area as well, and most middle-state Federalists were moving away from their initial free trade policy toward protectionism. The building of national roads and canals favored the development of these areas, which was fundamental to Federalist theory, and Clay, and the Whigs. This Ohio old frontier was also similar to Clay's Kentucky congressional district. The Whigs, after collecting old Federalists into their party, were the driving force in the industrialization of the United States.

Few dreamt that it would be a young Whig, Abraham Lincoln, who idolized Henry Clay, who would set a Republican protectionist policy that would last over sixty years. Lincoln went out of his way to promote domestic manufacturing even with the pressing needs of the Union. It was a precedent that defined manufacturing policy for a young Republican Party. In the 1870s, the torch was passed to future president James Garfield, who headed the Ways and Means Committee that enforced trade policy. Garfield groomed William McKinley to take over the Ways and Means Committee under Garfield's presidency.

The real peak of scientific protectionism came with the passage of the McKinley Tariff of 1890. The Tariff Bill of 1890 was the career signature of William McKinley, and it would give him national support and a local defeat. What at first was called his Waterloo would actually forge his sword of victory. The Fifty-first Congress of 1888 formed with what was believed to be a mandate for tariff reform. The Republicans controlled the

White House and both branches of the legislature. Providence seemed to favor McKinley, and McKinley's power was peaking. The tariff issue, now preeminent, was what McKinley had studied his whole life. Prior to the McKinley administration, although not a personal friend of McKinley, President Benjamin Harrison had supported high tariffs. McKinley drew on old friends such as ex-president Hayes for advice. McKinley showed true brilliance in his compromises and teamwork, not only in the House but also with the Senate and White House. He was dealing with a mix in both parties. The tariff bill included many innovations that helped farmers and manufacturers. It was an extremely well prepared bill discussing industry and production statistics. The bill completed the evolutionary steps of American tariffs from revenue generating to protective to industry development. Yes, there would be a small increase in prices initially, but prices would actually decrease long term as industry invested in research and development because of stable prices. It was a pleasant surprise that long-term market stability provided by tariffs should actually improve investment. McKinley went further, establishing a congressional commission to assure any profits from tariffs were put into plant investment.

McKinley's Bill of 1890 used science and statistics to apply the tariff rates. First, McKinley argued that the revenue tariff approach was the real problem, not protective tariffs. His statistics were convincing: "Before 1820 nearly all our imports were dutiable; scarcely any were free; while in 1824 the proportion of free imports was less than 6 percent; in 1830, about 7 percent.... The percent of free imports from 1873 to 1883 was about 30 percent, and under the tariff revision of 1883 it averaged 33 percent."[1] For his 1890 bill, it would be 50 percent. The difference was that it focused on addressing the nation's needs, not on taxing revenue production — which for years had been the major source of government income. The plan was fully consistent with the Federalists' view of a manufacturing utopia. The McKinley plan was a result of years of study, and no one knew more about tariffs than McKinley; but he would have to make political compromises to get the bill passed. McKinley pored nightly over the tariff schedules and surveyed his colleagues on industry needs.

McKinley argued that protective tariffs had not restricted exports, and again the numbers supported him:

---

1 William McKinley, " The Value of Protection," *The North American Review*, June 1890, Volume 150, Issue 403, pages 747-48

We sell to Europe $449,000,000 worth of products and buy $208,000,000 worth. We sell to North America to the value of $9,645,000 and buy $5,182,000. We sell to South America $13,810,000 and buy $9,088,000.[1]

McKinley was not alone in is his evaluation. Bismarck in 1882 had hailed the US protective tariffs: "[I]t is my deliberate judgment that the prosperity of America is mainly due to its system of protective laws."[2] The McKinley tariffs were focused on building America, not restricting trade. They were applied in a manner that did not produce trade wars. Still, McKinley was clear that his tariffs were nationalistic: "The free-trader wants the world to enjoy with our citizens equal benefits of trade in the United States. The Republican protectionist would give the first chances to our people, and would so levy duties upon the products of other nations as to discriminate in favor of our own."[3]

McKinley's extensive study had brought scientific management into tariff rates, but Congress preferred politics to science. A tariff commission was also established to monitor the impact of the tariffs. This regulatory committee helped the opposition assure fairness and companies invested in jobs, not filling their pockets. And it wasn't just manufacturing that benefited. A 40 percent tariff on pickles allowed the rise of the great Heinz Company of Pittsburgh.

The years of the McKinley tariffs saw America overtake Britain in steel production and productivity. American glass did the same. Great companies like Westinghouse, General Electric, Ford Motor, United States Steel, Goodrich Rubber, Firestone, Goodyear, AT&T, Bell Telephone, John Deere, Libbey Glass, and many others became internationally dominant. This was the era of the Chicago World's Fair in 1893, which would herald the rise of US manufacturing to world prominence. This was the era of paternal capitalism that built many of the nation's great cities such as Akron, Toledo, Pittsburgh, Detroit, Chicago, Cleveland, St. Louis, Buffalo, Trenton, and Wheeling. McKinley's view saw tariffs as helping big business and working men both. It was national capitalism pure and simple. And McKinley, for his part, built an unusual political alliance of workers and businessmen. It was nationalism and required a centric view of America. It was also rooted in a type of isolationism. It had its faults and weaknesses, but it delivered a "full lunch pail." It was a period of prosperity and hope. Workers' conditions and environmental conditions could have been better, but it is a clear contrast to the devas-

1 Ibid.
2 Ibid.
3 Ibid.

tation of de-industrialization that followed. The biggest problem with de-industrialization is not even the losses of income, homes, and family; it destroys even hope.

The great cities built by tariffs and McKinley's national capitalism have been leveled by de-industrialization. Most of our large cities have been affected to some degree. The survivor cities like Pittsburgh and Boston have traded industry for universities, hospitals, and government as the largest employers. Even these few bright spots have lost a substantial tax base and neighboring areas of poverty. Efforts in most industrial cities to somehow replace the rubber, glass, steel, and auto factories have resulted in frustration and failure. Devastated industrial cities like Detroit, Youngtown, Cleveland, Trenton, Flint, and Buffalo have become black holes to sink social services funds into. Even the few Americans at Mont Pèlerin could not have envisioned the devastation.

De-industrialization is too often studied in terms of straw man villains. Management is blamed for its lack of modernization and investment. Owners are blamed for their greed. Unions are blamed for their excess wages and benefit demands; government for its inability to act and for over-regulation. Many parties overreact in the quest for a pristine environment or need to maximize profits. Our economists and politicians speak of "creative destruction" wherein the loss of manufacturing jobs is necessary but can be compensated for through endless re-training for high tech career alternatives ... that never materialize. We see corruption in industry and government and say it is deserved, but don't see the relationship to the national lack of moral education. Business schools have long ago dropped ethics courses. We point the finger and blame others. Yet we are all to blame. Capitalism requires both government regulation and a moral compass.

De-industrialization is the result of our long-running failure to implement a national industrial policy. The United States is missing the national economic vision of Alexander Hamilton, Henry Clay, or William McKinley and the political leadership on industrial growth shown by Abraham Lincoln or William McKinley. We have convinced ourselves that trade can truly be free between varying different national goals. We had adopted a single economic philosophy as natural law and have eliminated debate. We have priced in paternal costs such as health care and pensions into our products and then try to trade freely with nations that don't ask their industries to help support social costs. We accept huge trade imbalances as part of free trade. We point to minor improvements in exports and ignore the flood of imports. We have bought a vision of a nation that is post-manufacturing and post-industrial. We favor a large international banking system versus a community-based one.

The large international banking system was a major premise in the Mont Pèlerin vision of the world. Free trade was to be fueled by interlocking international banks with the American dollar as the standard currency. New York would (and did) ascend to the ruling seat of the world's banking system. This was the same vision of J. P. Morgan and international bankers in 1890s. Morgan's vision had been blocked for almost a century by Republican protectionist policies going back to Abraham Lincoln and the former Whig Party. It is tempting to blame the banks, but they too were allowed to become international, in allegiance to the Mont Pèlerin international philosophy that had been accepted nationwide.

The great years of manufacturing had its roots with Abraham Lincoln and continued to the late 1920s. It had a brief renaissance in the 1950s. In fairness, the glory years of manufacturing were not glorious for everybody. The pollution of those days would have shocked most today. Work was available, but it was hard work. Immigrant workers struggled in dirty boarding rooms and shanty neighborhoods, but on average they spent less than a generation in those conditions. Wages, while considered low in this country, were the envy of the world. The American industrial worker made five to ten times the wages of his counterpart in Europe. It was those wages, in part, that attracted immigrants to this nation. In addition, these workers whose beliefs were unpopular in their home countries found religious liberty here. There were indeed biases, racism, religious intolerance, and class division in industrial America; but on the whole, performance determined one's rise in industry. Rags-to-riches stories were common. Many injustices in society were addressed, albeit slowly at times. Education was the quest of the people, not the government. People pulled themselves up without any safety nets except those offered by the community itself. Even the concept of life- and disability-insurance evolved out of immigrants' fraternal organizations. Rarely was hope missing. For most people, factory work was not a destiny but a gateway to the American dream.

Another part of the story that is lost is how de-industrialization has affected the middle class managers, sons and daughters of the workers who built those factories under Republican protectionism of the early 1900s. The fact is that the factories of the late 1800s and early 1900s expanded the middle class. Often, studies looked at the mill worker's son who took a similar job at the mill; but it was also common for a son or daughter to take a white-collar job in the local factory. Between 30 and 40 percent of low-level workers moved into higher-level jobs during their lifetimes in the Carnegie Steel mills. Even more telling was the upward mobility between generations, with 40 percent of blue-collar sons moving to white-collar work. Then the next generation of mill workers routinely sent their children to college. "Management," often blamed for the downfall of the rubber and steel industries, were members of the same communities and families as the workers. Often the top executives came from these worker roots. There was a love of the industry they worked in, and they liked the workers. They were all proud. This was the nature of paternal capitalism; it was family oriented. Similarly, the bars and stores in these industrial cities were owned by second- or third-generation factory workers.

Another fact, rarely written about, is that while steel workers and rubber workers did not enjoy such benefits as disability insurance and pensions, the paternal system did help. Under the great barons like Firestone and Carnegie, disabled workers were often given light duty work to ease them toward retirement. Henry Ford built factories to employ the disabled. Immigrant workers were able to form their own insurance pools. Even as the unions demanded and won improved benefit packages, and the paternal practice of helping disabled workers lasted into the 1970s. Free trade would, in many ways, bring an end to paternal capitalism.

The free trade ideas of the post-war world would be the poisoned seeds of America's de-industrialization. The results would not be seen until the 1970s. Post-war American industry was a return to the golden years of the 1890s. In the 1950s factories no longer had to offer upward mobility, since manufacturing jobs now provided a middle-class income. These now high-paying jobs fueled prosperity in cities like Pittsburgh, Cleveland, Detroit, Akron, and Youngstown and into the suburbs. Workers' sons and daughters filled the expanded state colleges in the 1960s. Company scholarships got many of them into private colleges as well. Malls and small businesses sprouted to service these middle class families. Tax bases expanded, funding improved communities and school districts. Dentists, doctors, and opticians (many of them, too, the sons and daughters of workers) increased in tandem with the increasing benefits of these factory workers. Southern resorts grew as workers and their families took bigger and longer vacations.

Meanwhile, the victory of Mont Pèlerin concepts in universities and government was hardly noticed. American industry seemed invincible.

The real concern was the alleged evolving industrial–government complex. General Motors seemed to own government. But already during the 1960s things were changing. De-industrialization would start by the end of the decade. Its start, a sudden drop, was first attributed to the normal business cycle. De-industrialization is merely running this prosperity tape backward. It was not the first wave of de-industrialization seen in America, but it was the first one that struck at the national level.

CHAPTER 3. AMERICA'S FIRST DE-INDUSTRIALIZATION

While all industry in the US experienced the ups and downs of the business cycle, the first effects of actual de-industrialization were seen already in the 1940s. New England's textile industry was the first to show a true pattern of de-industrialization at the regional level. New England's iconic textile mills had seen their share of ups and downs, but a different pattern began before World War II. The textile industry found itself in a highly competitive global market. Much of it moved out of New England in search of a way to reduce costs. New England's de-industrialization was regional, with mills moving to the South where wages were lower. The industry would battle during the Great Depression and survive for a short war boom in the 1940s.

The de-industrialization of New England was different from today's devastation. It was an internal American trend, a movement related only to specific regions and industries, unlike the broad, national problem we face today. Yet the fundamentals were the same. The roots go back to 1900 with the usual suspects: high labor cost, cheap imports, high taxes, government regulation, and lack of plant modernization. Like all de-industrialization events, it was also the result of a decision that had at least tacit approval from the government.

The very success of textile workers in winning higher wages and better working conditions made them uncompetitive with workers in other locations. Similarly, state governments started to require improved working conditions but soon they were over-regulating, on a competitive basis with other locations.

Not surprisingly, de-industrialization began where the industrialization of America started — the New England textile industry. The New England textile industry had been born out of the British naval blockade during the War of 1812. Francis Cabot Lowell and 11 other Boston shipping men started to produce multipurpose cloth as a new business. The Boston Manufacturing Company became America's first integrated factory in 1813. On a visit to England, Lowell had memorized the parts of British looms, which were not allowed to be shipped to America for decades. He was able to re-create the automated looms back in the United States. The business took off as demand for fabric surged during the British blockade.

The New England textile industry became a model for productivity and found a creative way to reduce labor costs. New England had a labor shortage, and the industry turned to women to "man" the factories. They paid the highest wages to women in the United States, but still, at the time, they were half the wages men were paid. The average stay for young women was about four years, as they would leave work to start a family. They had to attract these women in a Puritan society which didn't embrace the notion of women working outside the home. They adjusted to that by creating a unique brand of paternal capitalism. The women were housed in well-kept boardinghouses with many benefits such as education. Health care was provided. The women with their wages built strong communities around the mills. New England towns such as Lowell were centers of local commerce and education. These towns had the earliest of America's circulating libraries. The textile mills were never to be manned by a permanent under-class as in Europe, where there was no means to escape one's lot.

The industry from its earliest days thrived on the protection provided by Henry Clay's legislation and the American System of tariffs. Henry Clay was more popular in New England than in his home state of Kentucky. Without any protection, the New England textile industry never would have gotten off the ground in a world where the British had a monopoly on textiles. Even without high tariffs, by the 1840s, New England was beginning to be able to compete with the highly unionized British factories. Americans began to develop better textile machines. England had banned the importation of automated textile machines and skilled machine makers to the United States, but New England mechanics were able to overcome the ban. Skilled mechanics left Europe regardless of the ban to get higher paying jobs in America. Even machines were smuggled out of England for Yankee mechanics to reverse engineer. The advent of American-made machines created a new machine-tool industry throughout the Connecticut Valley.

The British textile industry was experiencing the destruction of the hand crafts and guild system in the 1810s due to automation, as steam-driven looms were replacing weavers all over Europe. Over 700,000 skilled weavers would be put out of work in a few decades. Handloom weavers had moved from a peak of 100,000 in Scotland in 1800 to 84,560 in 1840, and 25,000 by 1850. Automated industrialization eliminated the weaver craft entirely. The weavers had been upper middle class crafts-men and were considered the aristocrats of the crafts. But the early appli-cation of automation had given England a major cost advantage. Mean-while, the use of tariffs for several decades gave the New England textile industry a chance to adapt to and compete with the new automation.

The de-crafting of Europe would result in major revolutions by 1850, but even earlier workers (in this case craftsmen) took to the streets with violence. The shift to automation brought fear to these craftsmen. Linen weavers had been on the leading edge of the first wave of global industri-alization and were known for their radical resistance to the automation. In England, what became known as the Luddite movement had chal-lenged the elimination of the skilled craft weavers. Factories and equip-ment were burned as the Luddites hid in nearby Sherwood Forest.

The collapse of the weaver crafts guild forced out-of-work families to immigrate to America. America embraced these craft immigrants but also embraced the new technology, moving from craftsmen to "skilled workers." Labor-short America was able to pay high wages compared to Europe, even while embracing automation. The work system changed to highly-automated manufacture. Ironically, many sons of these immi-grants, such as Andrew Carnegie, would take America to an even more automated production system. William Carnegie, father of Andrew, was one of the very elite "damask" weavers who specialized in complex and intricate designs. This specialization allowed damask weavers to buck the trend of automation longer, but even so many of them migrated to America in the 1840s. William Carnegie brought his family to Pittsburgh to work in the booming cotton mills. Andrew Carnegie would see his father die depressed, unable to embrace the automation. Andrew Carn-egie would vow not to follow in his father's footsteps. Taking a laborer job in a Pittsburgh cotton mill, Andrew would rise to automate the steel industry and become one of America's richest industrialists. While almost eliminating skilled labor, Carnegie's automation created unskilled labor jobs far beyond the ability of the nation to fill them.

America had taken a lead in both automation and production by the 1840s. Given protection, the New England textile quality won over other parts of the nation with its high quality. America would not, however, adopt the old guild unions of Europe. European immigrants helped fill the demand for unskilled and skilled workers in the textile mills. Still, some of the American productivity edge came from the 75-hour work week and pushy supervisors. Automation had brought its own set of new problems. The 12-hour days provoked sufficient push-back that a national movement formed, which eventually led to 10-, then 8-hour days.

The factory was a new entity for workers and far different than the fresh air of the farm. Factories were dark, noisy, and dangerous. People from outside the factory held two distinct views. There was one group that almost worshipped technology and machines. Another saw the factory system as oppressive and de-humanizing. The workers fell somewhere in between. They liked the money and the freedom it brought, particularly the women of the New England textile industry. Those workers who could not tolerate the manufacturing environment knew it almost immediately. For those who stayed, a few years of money, freedom, and education seemed to be worth the unpleasant environment.

After the Civil War, industry was under attack for providing poor working conditions and health and safety issues. Government and unions gained influence, and the workers' pay and conditions improved — but at a cost to the manufacturers. Local government and state added more regulation and taxes. By the late 1890s, many of the mills were in need of major renovation. Still, the attitude remained that the textile industry was here to stay. Labor, however, remained in short supply in New England. High-paying wages in the steel and railroad industries drew most of the immigrant labor to other locations. Still, textile workers were well paid compared to those in other nations.

Just prior to the beginnings of de-industrialization, New England textile workers had achieved much in wages and benefits. By the start of World War I, the textile industry remained highly competitive internationally, but it lacked the weight of the steel industry. The protectionism of the 1800s was reduced substantially as competition rose from inside and outside America. The textile mills were old, and new technology had been invented that required these mills to modernize. The old guild system and 1840s socialist movement of Europe had morphed in America's trade unions. Work conditions and pay improved, but costs became higher than those of foreign competitors. For the first time, America's technology did not keep pace with the output of cheap international labor. Labor costs now became central to overall costs again. The mills, however, looked South to where there was less union influence, lower cost labor, and less government regulation. New England became the first region to face a new type of de-industrialization. The good news for the nation was that the textile industry did re-create itself in the South with non-union labor and lower taxes. The American South of the 1920s offered some of the advantages of China today.

The next manufacturing center to be de-industrialized after New England was Trenton, New Jersey. Trenton, more than any other American city, represented a center of manufacturing diversity. The de-industrialization of Trenton in the late 1950s and early 1960s may have been the herald of things to come. This again was a movement within America; the driving factors were similar to the New England textile industry, with two exceptions. One element that might be considered exceptional was the number of corporate mergers taking place that resulted in the closing or reduction of local plants. The other was a decline of the economic weight of Trenton's inner city, something that usually occurs after de-industrialization. Still, this early urban decline may have played a role in later in accelerating de-industrialization but was hidden by bigger events in cities like Detroit, Akron, and Cleveland. Trenton represented the front line of the post-war globalization campaign. Manufacturing, trying to compete, moved west and south to reduce taxes and get cheaper, more cooperative labor.

The exact formula many had suggested for cities like Detroit and Akron, yet Trenton would fall before the others. Trenton made steel, rubber, pottery, and electrical components. It ranked only behind Akron in rubber. Trenton was a product of the pro-tariff Republican polices of the time of the McKinley era. Trenton's road to industrialization began in the late 1800s with industrial pottery factories. By the 1890s, Trenton was the leading manufacturer of sanitary ware and electrical porcelain. Another entrepreneur, John Lenox, rose from potter to capitalist. Lenox moved into high end porcelain but Japanese and world competition almost destroyed him. The local Republican Party took up his cause, imposing tariffs to allow the company to grow. Over the years, Lenox not only grew nationally but expanded into international markets.

Trenton also had a long history in iron and steel production. One of America's first industrialists, Peter Cooper, started Trenton Iron Works that produced wrought iron beams for city buildings. The famous Roebling brothers set up their steel wire mill in Trenton to make cable for the building of the Brooklyn Bridge. In 1911, United States Steel of Pittsburgh bought some of the mills to make steel wire. Interestingly, this purchase by New York and Pittsburgh companies would be the start of de-industrialization of Trenton.

The third leg of Trenton's major industry was rubber products. In the 1870s, five companies in Trenton obtained rights from Charles Goodyear to start producing rubber products, initially, products like belts, shoes, and rubberized cloth. By the turn of the century, more rubber companies emerged in Trenton to make bicycle and automotive tires. The rubber industry grew rapidly into the 1920s and rivaled Akron with over 8,000 rubber workers. Several of the rubber executives rose in the Republican Party, which protected the industry from European manufacturers. By the 1930s, Thermoid was the city's largest rubber company. The success of rubber, steel, and pottery led to a major union movement of the CIO in the late 1930s, in Trenton and most of America's industrial cities. Trenton became a union stronghold, which would limit the expansion of the local industries in preference to building in the non-union South. Akron, Ohio would suffer the same fate.

In the 1950s, most of Trenton's industries were purchased by non-local corporations. The failing city infrastructure put a brake on investment. The city's largest employer, Roebling's Sons, faced a unique set of circumstances. It was a family-owned company, but inheritance taxes and the need for more capital made it impossible to stay family-owned. The company officers sold the company to Colorado Fuel and Iron in 1953; and by 1963, all the Trenton operations were closed down. Roebling's Sons had been losing money after the war, as had many of the Trenton's factories. In 1953, the downtown of Trenton was suffering from the loss in revenue from corporate taxes and reduced population, exacerbated by the trend to move to the suburbs. National magazines started to publish articles on the poor condition of the city. A 1957 *House and Home* article predicted that in 25 years Trenton would be a "nightmarish, ethnic, low income ghetto." [1]

The decline of downtown manufacturing started in the 1950s as jobs moved to the suburbs and to the South. One reason was the success of unions, which helped workers in the immediate short run but, by taking wages and benefits to uncompetitive highs, drove corporation to move the jobs out altogether. The South was empowered by the passage of

---

1 John T. Cumbler, *A Social History of Economic Decline*, (New Brunswick: Rutgers University Press, 1989), p. 159

the Taft-Hartley Act of 1947 which allowed states to pass right-to-work laws. Trenton industrial workers, New England textile workers, and New York garment workers were hit first.

Large cities suffered from de-industrialization for a number of reasons. Trenton of the 1950s would be the ghost of America's future. For Trenton, it was a spiral of less tax income for government-run schools, roads and other essentials, declining infrastructure, and falling real estate values. As the new owners looked to expand their operations, Trenton's image made it unpopular. Executives and managers as individuals and as companies found few positive reasons to remain or build in Trenton. Its strong unions also made it a poor place to expand plants. The city lacked some of the strong arts and cultural assets that had at least slowed the decline of other cities. Trenton's factories moved south, many workers left, and poor Southern blacks moved into what was essentially ghetto housing in the early 1960s.

As manufacturing jobs dropped off and unemployment rose, wives took jobs in the service and government industries to pay household bills. Increasing, services actually expanded local and state government in the 1950s and 1960s. This helped ease the pain, since Trenton was a state capital. Schools and government spending were out of sync with the actual decline of manufacturing, and the bill would come due a decade later. By 1960 in Trenton, more people worked in government than in manufacturing. The problem with government jobs is that to pay for them, one has to draw more taxes from a shrinking tax base. In the 1970s and 1980s, state government looked to save downtown Trenton by building offices and government buildings. The aging unemployed and the lack of industry further strained the government's safety net. Being laid-off in your 50s was (and is) generally the end of a career. The homeless and underemployed became a permanent part of the city, requiring even more government help. As Southern blacks moved to Trenton to compete for fewer jobs, race tensions increased. Trenton would mark the path followed by many cities by the 1980s. For many Americans, the world was turned upside down.

American labor history is one of struggle, but for a few decades it gave workers the world's best health care and retirement benefits. Both union and management should get credit (and protection) for their efforts. These well-earned and deserved benefits are part of American product costs, making it impossible for us to compete with cheap foreign labor.

We had developed a means to finance world class health care, only to trade it for free trade. In the end, expanding industry would be a better solution to the health care issues of today. Tariffs at least would have protected the differences in health care and pensions between "free" traded products. This new international approach does a disservice not only to our workers but to exploited workers in other countries. Under free trade, foreign countries where labor is paid less — and lacks the benefits Americans have come to expect — creates incentives for factories to relocate abroad.

CHAPTER 4. A NEW WORLD ORDER

The post-World War world is far different than the world prior. A global division and competition in ideology between communism and capitalism often dominated the news and American psyche, but it made little difference to industrial America. Initially, after World War II, America was the only game in town, dominating in steel, auto, rubber, and durable goods manufacture. The adoption of the Mont Pèlerin Society's economic philosophy meant little while the competition from Germany, the rest of Europe, and Japan were in ruins. Peace, the United Nations; and Western unity vis-à-vis the rest of the world took priority over trade when it came to setting American policy. In any case, American industrial exports were robust as the world rebuilt. Nonetheless, the world order of Mont Pèlerin called for the decline of American prosperity. America's steel industry was to feel it first.

In 1947, the United States produced an amazing 57 percent of the world's steel. It was limited in exports by the booming domestic market it had to supply. American money, however, flowed quickly into the rebuilding of the world. The first sign of a future slowdown for American industry was in exports. By 1960, United States accounted for 26 percent of the world's steel production, and Japan was the world's leader in steel exports. This was a silent change. The loss of exports hardly seemed like a crisis; Americans were happy to dominate the domestic market. The problem became more acute for the steel industry in the 1970s.

Steel production was a massive employment tool for governments and their economies. Just a few decades after their demolition, countries like Japan, Russia, and Germany were producing much more steel than needed for their own domestic consumption. The steel industry, because of its potential to supply thousands of jobs, was highly subsidized by foreign governments.[1] These export-steel dependent manufacturers were applauded by world economic organizations, which saw it as a means of de-arming the militaries of many aggressive nations. In addition, third-world countries saw the same advantages in developing their own steel industries. American manufacturers were content to supply the more stable American market.

But that stable market was disrupted by a challenge from imports. Favorable free trade laws, new foreign mills and equipment, and massive investment by American banks into Japanese mill expansion paved the way. Steel lost ground on several import fronts besides direct steel imports. Imported cars, capital goods, durable goods, and equipment all took away from the American mills' steel business. America was caught with high wages and benefits from the prosperity of the 1960s. Japanese steel companies were supported by their own government. America was also constrained by turn-of-the-century anti-trust polices, which limited its ability to compete with Japanese government-backed monopolies. But most important was a basic shift in government philosophy that had taken away tariffs as a means to level the playing field.

The world vision of the first meeting of the Mont Pèlerin Society had come to pass. There have been some positive aspects to "free trade," such as the fall of the Soviet Union and communism. The world had avoided a world conflict. It had come at an economic cost to all Americans through de-industrialization.

Probably the least talked about attribute of de-industrialization is the loss of family, community, and even nation. The Social Welfare Institute of Boston College defined the biggest characteristic of de-industrialization like this: "What de-industrialization ignores is that 'people want to improve their community.' An unfettered investment policy destroys communities and personal assets while it creates an 'industrial refuge' crisis of serious proportion — whole subcommunities without life space or work. Ultimately, the process of creative destruction is sustainable, as Joseph Schumpeter [Mont Pèlerin] himself reluctantly admitted in

---

1 William T. Hogan, *World Steel in the 1980s*, (Lexington: Lexington Books, 1983), p. 204

sections of his classic work."[1] A simple ride through the downtowns of Detroit, Akron, Trenton, and others would eliminate any belief in creative destruction, the wonders of the post-industrial age, and the abundance of information-age jobs.

The rise of a strong steel industry in other countries was supported by the infrastructure of Mont Pèlerin economics, a world trade and banking system. The Mont Pèlerin Society's philosophy took hold in the postwar world so quickly because of its vision of a world banking structure. The banking industry always had a propensity to an international order and trade. There had been strong ties between J.P. Morgan in America and the Rothschilds for almost a hundred years. Banks could make money off trade while breaking down national economic boundaries. National capitalists such as Andrew Carnegie, Henry Ford, and others had always feared large New York-based banks for this reason.

The General Agreement on Tariffs and Trade in 1947 assured the freedom to fully implement the principles of the Mont Pèlerin Society. The General Agreement on Tariffs and Trade (GATT) was implemented by the Western nations after World War II to regulate trade and assure the world economic recovery and peace. It set the US dollar as the international currency and America as the leader in free trade. GATT also established the institutions of the World Bank and the International Monetary Fund. GATT would govern international trade from 1947 until 1995 when the World Trade Organization (WTO) replaced it formally. GATT guiding principles, however, remain in effect today.

The original GATT Treaty of 1947 and its 23 members tried to achieve fair trade through reciprocity and negotiated trade deals. The GATT reversed the American policy of scientific tariffs that had been the rule from the birth of the nation. GATT did aim for the reciprocity that William McKinley had added to his famous 1890 Tariff Act. At least in its stated mission, GATT was not "free" trade but the elimination of "discriminatory treatment" and "barriers to trade."

The original GATT required some reciprocity in trade, but this was never really enforced. In fact, America's rivals seemed excluded from the reciprocity agreements. Japan's steel industry grew from less than a million tons a year in 1947 to 119 million tons in 1973. Japan was making steel at 30 million tons over its domestic needs. The Japanese auto industry was similarly moving from one million vehicles in 1963 to over eleven million in 1980, again far beyond domestic needs. Politicians argued that

---

1 Barry Bluestone and Bennett Harrison, *The Deindustrialization of America*, (New York: Basic Books, 1982), p. 20

the International Trade Commission stood as a protector of fair trade, knowing it had a bias against America. The International Trade Commission often ruled against US companies, arguing it was a labor cost issue. Anything that distributed manufacturing away from the US was considered a positive. Dumping low-priced goods on the American market was almost encouraged.

The GATT would later address "anti-dumping" practices, which had first been used by the British with iron products after the War of 1812. While trade after GATT still remained a type of economic chess game, it did lead to a remarkable amount of trade liberalization between nations. American jobs were clearly being traded for peace and a united front against communism. GATT was a negotiation-based multilateral instrument more than a formal treaty, but it became an all controlling entity regardless of its classification. Most considered it a de facto international organization. GATT was a series of eight "rounds" of meetings starting in 1947 in Geneva and ending in Uruguay in 1986. These "rounds" lasted from 5 months to 87 months in duration. The rounds produced unique sets of agreements and tariff levels. The Kennedy round (1964–1967) resulted in a 35 percent reduction in tariff rates between members, which is the largest in the history of the world.

The GATT has been open to debate, but little else. It has controlled trade rules from 1947 to this day. Labor has questioned whether these tariff-free arrangements have enforced lower wages in the industrial countries. It is a key political issue, which many call "fair trade." The question centers on countries like the United States, where product prices reflect pensions, healthcare, and living wages, competing against products of countries such as China and India, where these worker benefits are lacking. Many Americans argue that the World Trade Organization has resulted in loss of sovereignty. An ongoing debate continues over intellectual rights and the use of agricultural subsidies. More recently, environmental issues have been part of the discussions. Again, environmental costs of production processes can put responsible producers at a disadvantage compared to countries with fewer regulations.

A major ancillary effect of the GATT was an international unity and interlocking ties between the world's banks. It has reduced America to just-another-country status, except that America was left to foot the bill to maintain the peace. America passed from nationalism to internationalism, and from isolationism to the world's policeman.

Both American and Japanese banks would supply the necessary capital in Japan for a manufacturing miracle. By 1949, Japan had rebuilt its steel mills and reached pre-war levels. Banks and political leaders saw steel as the core to a new economy as it provided so many high paying jobs. By lowering costs and improving quality, Japan by 1957 was the world's foremost industry with steelmaking capacity far beyond domestic needs. The international environment of free trade put them in a position to capitalize further. By 1964, a leading industrial analyst noted that "28 percent of Japan's steel exports was going to America. In Japan, a thrust into followed closely upon the success in steel; by 1965, Japan had replaced Britain as the world's leading shipbuilding nation."[1]

Maybe the biggest problem was that America was a house divided against itself. It was industry and government divided against itself. The auto companies wanted auto tariffs but resisted steel tariffs so they could obtain cheap steel for car building. The two political parties played labor against management. Management pointed to unions and unions pointed to managers. American economists argued that free trade was the best thing for American capitalism, when the results showed the opposite. American banks favored free trade and helped finance foreign competition. American political leaders traded American jobs for international support. Environmentalists saw no room for compromise or phased improvement. In the end, academia, the banking moguls, and the intellectual class put out the message that order and security in this new world was worth the sacrifice of our industrial assets. The final sign of this new order was the collapse of the American auto industry.

The first signs of this came in the 1950s. The story of the rise of Japanese imports and Toyota in America really is one of America's entrance into the global economy. The first sale of the Toyota Toyopet in 1958 hardly started a flood of imports; in fact, the Toyopet proved unsuccessful in the American market. America's first Toyota dealer was in San Francisco. Toyopet opened its offices in Hollywood more as a statement than as a functioning headquarters. These first few car imports targeted a niche in the market. This had been a pre-war goal of Japanese automakers. In 1936, the Japanese government passed the Automobile Manufacturing Industries Act with the express purpose of breaking the US car monopoly. Toyota and Datsun had taken the lead prior to the war and now they took up the old goals. A small but growing import market arose in post-war America with the entrance of the Volkswagen Beetle, which started in 1949. While the sale of a Toyota was hardly noticed by the American press, it was a strategic project, not a tactical move. To the

---

1 David Halberstam, *The Reckoning*, (New York: Avon Books, 1987), p. 276

Japanese it was guerilla warfare, like Apple and Microsoft working quietly in the shadow of giant IBM. Toyota was taking a long view toward becoming a major player in America, but the plan was difficult from a product standpoint.

The Toyopet had a top speed of just 55 mph and a small 27 horsepower engine. When the Toyopet bombed in the United States, Toyota took it off the market and had it redesigned. Toyota was considered a joke in America and was only producing 60,000 cars a year in Japan. But Toyota proved flexible, against the odds. The idea of testing, redesigning for a specific model, and eventually localizing production became its business model as a global company. General Motors in 1959 was completely unconcerned by this. General Motors had the US government to worry about.

General Motors was the world's largest auto company and the most profitable in 1959. It had 52 percent of the US market share. In 1956, the Senate alleged that General Motors used monopolistic practices. The Justice Department warned of extreme action to break up General Motors if they didn't reduce their presence. The government threats forced General Motors to expand internationally and diversify nationally. Yet, with all the pressure, General Motors did roll out a small car of its own and a potential import fighter, the Chevy Corvair, in 1959. The Corvair was popular, but was seen as less safe than the bigger, traditional models of the day; and the size of General Motors Corporation made it a target for safety activists.

The Corvair had an air-cooled engine and rear-wheel drive which challenged the popular import — the Volkswagen Beetle. The rear air-cooled engine greatly improved fuel economy and ride quality. The car had many revolutionary design elements and was named Motor Trend Car of the Year for 1960. It was also on a 1960 cover of Time Magazine, which hailed its engineering. Even with all the safety concerns, the Corvair proved highly successful, selling 1.8 million cars in the decade of the 1960s. In the first four years, the Corvair was hit with over 100 lawsuits, but these remained below the public's radar until 1965 with the publication of Ralph Nader's *Unsafe at Any Speed*. The early lawsuits provided the original research material for his book. Rader's advising role to Congress on car safety also allowed him access to the overview of the national safety problem.

The major impact of his book would be the unanimous passage of the 1966 National Traffic and Motor Vehicle Safety Act. The Act addressed the rising fatalities and injuries of the 1960s. The Act represented a major shift in safety responsibility from the individual consumer to the federal government. The Act forced auto makers to add features such as safety belts and stronger shatter-resistant windshields. General Motors and the American auto makers stopped producing smaller cars.

In the late 1950s, the size of Toyota's and Nissan's small cars offered little threat to the big luxury market of the United States. Toyota struggled, even with an attractive price. The failure of the Toyoda model inspired the development of the Toyota Corona for the American market in 1964. The Corona was a six-passenger car with lower price tag, higher quality, and better gas mileage than the sedans of the Big Three. In 1965, Toyota Corona sales were just 6,400 vehicles; but by 1967, sales reached 71,000 vehicles and continued to double every year to 1971. With a growing reputation for quality, Toyota introduced the Crown, a semi-luxury car. In 1969, Toyota imported the Corolla, which would become the best import seller and America's favorite small car. By 1973, Toyota had hurt Volkswagen even more than the Big Three. The Big Three still considered the Japanese to be addressing a niche market, albeit a growing one. One overlooked factor was the improving Japanese quality and declining American quality, which was noticed by young upscale buyers. And the major advantage of good gas mileage meant less in times of cheap oil prices.

THE EFFECTS OF RISING FUEL PRICES

The big breakthrough for the small car market, where the Japanese were dominant, came with the oil crisis in 1973, when OPEC imposed an oil embargo and the cost of oil increased 70 percent. The root cause was the rising power of the Organization of Petroleum Exporting Countries (OPEC), controlled by Arab countries, to use oil as a political force. For decades, American oil companies had controlled Mideast oil countries like American colonies. The area was a political nightmare even then, with conflicts between Israel and the Arab countries. American control began to erode and strong nationalist leaders began to appear (from self-styled kings to elected officials to military dictators). In Libya, an anti-Israel radical named Muammar Qaddafi took over the government in 1969. Qaddafi took on the oil companies and was able to get 30 cents a barrel increase. The move emboldened OPEC and it was able to raise the price to $3 a barrel in 1971.

The industrialized nations were indeed dependent on Arab oil producers. The United States support of the Israeli military in the Yom Kippur War in October of 1973 created a political backlash in the Arab nations. Arab oil producing countries imposed an oil embargo on the United States and increased prices to its European allies by 70 percent. Oil jumped from $3 a barrel to over $5 a barrel overnight. By the end of the embargo, it had reached $11 a barrel. The United States relied on foreign countries for 36 percent of its oil in 1973. The embargo caused consumer panics, with stations running out of gas and mile-long lines. Rationing became necessary. Big cars were a major liability. The real problem had been growing for years. American dependence on foreign oil had increased through the 1960s from under 20 percent to 32 percent. Demand for oil was growing at 5 percent annually. About 7 percent of the oil by 1973 came from the Arab states. The root of the 1973 oil crisis goes back to the formation of OPEC in 1960 as a cartel to control supply and prices. The members by 1973 were Iran, Iraq, Kuwait, Saudi Arabia, Venezuela, United Arab Emirates, Qatar, Indonesia, Libya, Nigeria, and Algeria. OPEC was the supplier for 45 percent of the world market by 1973. The price of oil had remained around $1.00 a barrel for most of the 1960s and was $1.30 a barrel at the start of 1970. President Nixon's move of not allowing dollars to be converted to gold in 1971 caused a devaluation of the dollar, for which OPEC was unable to adjust. The inflation of the 1970s was putting pressure on OPEC to increase their prices, but it would be politics more than supply or demand that created the energy crisis. OPEC had for a decade proved ineffective in holding or raising prices due to the nature of cartel members to cheat. In 1967, OPEC had even failed with an embargo on the United States over the Six-Day War (Yom Kippur War).

On October 6, 1973, Syria and Egypt launched a surprise attack on Israel, beginning what became known as the Yom Kippur War. A week later the United States began an airlift to supply Israel in response to the supplying of Syria and Egypt by the Soviet Union. On October 16, OPEC raised the price of oil to $5.11 a barrel. The Arab states of OPEC announced that they would continue to increase the price of oil in five percent increments until their political goals were met. When Congress voted for a $2.2 billion relief package for Israel on October 20, the Arab states quickly announced a boycott against the United States. Oil prices rose to $12 a barrel and continued at this level through the 1970s. Prices at the pump went from 30 cents a gallon to $1.30 a gallon. The United States initially absorbed the impact with limited pain of higher prices. On November 5, the Arab states announced a 25 percent output cut, which started to put pressure on supplies in the United States.

The November output cut took the crisis to the main streets of the United States as gasoline station lines grew and reports of stations running out of gas created panics. President Nixon responded with a ban on Sunday gasoline sales, and daylight saving time was extended into winter to save fuel. Because consumers were topping off and keeping gas tanks full, odd-even sales days were implemented based on license plate numbers. Various other voluntary conservation moves were also implemented. Still, local panics occurred in highly populated areas. People often lacked gas to get to work. Carpooling became a necessity for many.

Secondary effects included a national trucker strike over the cost of fuel, and toilet paper panics based on oil shortages in the paper industry. Eventually the government imposed a 55 mph speed limit. Motorists were forced to wait in long lines and feared they'd run out of gas before getting to work, as gasoline supplies tightened. The government prepared to use ration coupons but never had to use the system, with the embargo ending in March of 1974.

The crisis caused a major market shift to small cars, a shift that would remain to some degree after the embargo ended. American manufacturers started to offer smaller cars, but quality issues hurt them. This allowed more Japanese auto manufacturers to gain a foothold in the market such as Nissan and Honda. The Japanese had lower labor costs, government support, and good products.

The oil embargo of 1973 changed everything for the American auto market. In that year, Volkswagen dominated American imports with more sales than Toyota and Nissan combined. But just as the oil crisis hit, Nissan had received the best car mileage rating by the Department of Transportation and private organizations, at 33 miles per gallon. In two years, both Toyota and Nissan overtook VW. The high valuation of the German mark also put VW in an uncompetitive advantage. Bad news for US producers: imports had jumped to 18 percent of the market, with Japanese supplying more than half of that. The oil crisis had saved Nissan, which had been failing in its sales.

The loss on the horizon for American manufacturing would change not only industry but the American working middle class. In the 1950s, typical manufacturing families had three children and lived in good but modest homes, often in the new suburbs of the period. These were one-income families in most cases. Mothers stayed home, except during the occasional strike, when they often found employment in retailing. To most of the country, living in often smoky and dirty cities or their outskirts, with polluted rivers, seemed hellish, but they saw only the surface.

The children of these workers didn't feel unprivileged but blessed. They lived in strong, vibrant ethnic communities. Family was the focus of their existence.

Children of these factory workers would have great memories of their childhoods. The year was marked with great holidays and celebrations such as Easter, Christmas, Halloween, graduations, First Communions, Memorial Day, the Fourth of July. There was the community fair for the various ethnic neighborhoods. Kids flooded to baseball games as their fathers worked in the mills and factories. Amusement parks were common for local entertainment. Community and grandparents played a key role in the lives of these kids as their fathers worked long hours in the factories. There was always someone to help out. Even funerals brought endless visits with food and helping hands. In cities like Pittsburgh and Cleveland, the slag industrial dumps of the mills offered days of fun sliding down the hills. There were weekend trips to the great museums, science centers, and libraries endowed by the paternal capitalists.

No child of factory workers dreamed of a better place to be. They had the new toy products coming on to the market. Christmas was special as the kids visited the city's major department store to find a full floor dedicated to toys. These toys included chemistry sets, erector sets, and trains reflecting American industry. Vacations often included the seashore, whether in New Jersey or the Carolinas, and maybe every fifth year a trip to Florida. Education was patriotic and moral-based as in previous decades. Churches, in particular Catholic churches of the workers in these industrial cities, were packed every Sunday. Communism was universally feared and denounced. Socialism was considered a gateway political system to communism. Most people were conservatives but voted Democratic. Both parties were somewhat conservative, and at least on American nationalism, could find agreement. The unions and management had their differences, but it was not framed in terms of class struggle as in Europe.

People knew their neighbors and church members, which formed a strong social network for all. Doctors made house calls. Police drove drunk drivers home. The paternal capitalists built or supported hospitals, churches, libraries, museums, and even social welfare centers. The workers had their neighborhood bars, churches, and fraternal organizations. Most social events were centered on family. Community street fairs and church festivals lasted a week. The major league baseball players often came to sign autographs. Unions held Christmas parties and Fourth of

July picnics for families. Ethnic roots were deep. The government was still trusted. Vietnam would soon change some of this.

Chapter 5. Lordstown, The Rouge, and Conneaut

The 1940s, 1950s, and 1960s saw the building of America's great citadels of industry in Henry Ford's massive and fully integrated car plant on the Rouge River, General Motor's Lordstown plant, then the re-consideration of United States Steel's Camelot steel mill at Conneaut, Ohio. These three plants were the dreams of a new type of global competition for America. The Ford Rouge plant made its own steel and glass. It was said it could produce a car in four days from raw materials such as iron ore, sand, limestone, and other basic materials. Lordstown was built in 1966 and was hailed as the quintessence of mass assembly in the world. Lordstown broke the 60-cars-an-hour record, producing 100 cars an hour using factory robots on a scale never seen before. Conneaut would be the dream left on the drawing board as the de-industrialization hit. A fully-integrated steel mill on Lake Erie at Conneaut, Ohio, had been a dream of Andrew Carnegie in 1898.

Ford would build his ultimate application of the assembly process at the River Rouge factory in the 1920s. The dream began in 1917. Henry Ford's vision included glassmaking, steelmaking, an iron foundry, a national railroad, machine shops, plastic molding department, and a massive assembly plant. Ford also planned to launch the building of the world's largest factory with almost no loans from banks. The Rouge operation would evolve over eight years of building, allowing Ford's managers to perfect new assembly methods. Ford visited daily, like Pharaoh overseeing its general construction, as his managers hammered out the details.

The Rouge plant was built in the Detroit suburb of Dearborn, next to Ford's Dearborn Estate and bird preserve. Ford chose the site to avoid Detroit taxes and regulation, but it was also to be America's first environmentally friendly plant. River Rouge would be America's citadel of industrial might, the assembly line, and vertical integration (owning the raw material supply chain) on an epic scale. By 1930, it would have 100,000 employees producing 4,000 cars a day from raw materials and would become the world's largest factory. The plant had its own railroad and over 100 miles of conveyors. Ford took glass and steelmaking to new efficiencies through integration. For example, Ford produced windshield glass at 20 cents a square foot versus 30 cents to $1.50 a square foot if purchased outside.[1]

Ford overcame every problem with bodacious solutions. When faced with a shortage of cement, he railroaded it in from New Jersey. He used Thomas Edison's cement casting system to expedite building. Ford also needed to build houses quickly for his growing workforce, so once again he applied the Edison cast cement method. The homes were considered ugly looking, but Ford was proud of the lumber-saving Edison approach. The Edison method used cast iron molds instead of wood framing for the cement. The cast iron mold could be used over and over while lumber was a onetime use and waste of lumber. The war, however, prevented the continued building of these cast houses. Still, Ford's Rouge Plant was the fore-runner of American manufacturing lean and green.

Ford wanted self-sufficiency in his manufacturing, and he demanded that his managers supply it. He made glass for less cost than his suppliers could do. Ford did the same for steelmaking at the Rouge. In fact, he created more cost reduction in the steelmaking process than Carnegie, since auto making was one of the largest sources of recyclable steel scrap. Ford even took the idea of recycling old cars to a new high at the Rouge. Dealers bought old cars, helping the buyer to purchase a new car. These old cars were sent to the Rouge, which had two production lines to deal with them. The newer cars went to one line for an overhaul and resale. The others went to a disassembly line, which dissembled and sorted parts for various scrap. Ford demonstrated an amazing system of overall recycling and reprocessing that is once again being studied by manufactur-

---

1 Charles Sorenson, *My Forty Years with Ford*, (Detroit: Wayne State University Press, 2006), p. 172

ers. Scrap wood was either re-sized or distilled into alcohol to drive his Model Ts.

Ford continued his war on waste at his Rouge plant, demanding the production and sale of by-products from steel and glass making. His coke plant, needed for the iron making blast furnaces, produced 20 million pounds of ammonium sulfate, which was sold as fertilizer. He used the coke by-product of benzol to run trucks in the plant. Ford even supplied benzol to Detroit area gas stations at a subsidized price for fuel in Model Ts. The coke plant also produced combustible coal gas for power generation. Ford distilled seven tons of garbage at his River Rouge plant daily to make alcohol, rivaling even the greenest manufacturers of today. He had a paper mill that used scrap wool, cloth, and paper to manufacture cardboard boxes. He used residue slag from iron and steelmaking to produce cinder cement blocks (many of which are still part of Detroit homes today). To keep his blast furnaces and steel plant running efficiently, he produced structural steel beams to sell. He recycled glass for his glass-making operation. Instead of burning off residue blast furnace gas, Ford used it to produce steam and electricity to run his machines.

The Rouge was also an innovation factory. Ford set up soybean oil processing plants at the Rouge River plant and the village industries at Milan and Saline. Ford was producing 500 tons of oil for use in car paints. These plants, in addition, were producing over 100 tons of oil, which was used as fluid in shock absorbers. Ford was replacing linseed oil in all his paints at a savings of over 35 percent to the cost of linseed oil, using about a half-gallon of soybean oil to paint a car and another half gallon for the car's shock absorbers. The remaining soybean cake was used in plastics and food items. At the Rouge, soybean plastics were used in distributor cases and electrical device covers. Ford was even mixing and pressing cellulose fiber and soybean cake into tractor seats. Ford used another 200,000 gallons of soybean oil for binder in his cast iron sand molds in the foundries. He was particularly proud of his soybean ice cream and flour as well. The flour was being used at the Ford bakery for employee cafeterias and grocery stores.

The Ford River Rouge continued to be the world's largest and most efficient plant into the 1950s. Ford had invested heavily in maintaining his first love. The speed of production at the Rouge would make it the center of unionization in the 1930s. Ford resisted the union, and this mistake led to violence in 1937 known as the "Battle of the Overpass." Still, the Rouge would be the iconic plant of the peak of American manufacturing. Paternal capitalism was practiced at a new level, with jobs for disabled workers and help for the unemployed. It was difficult to balance worker and company needs in a highly competitive environment, but the Rouge's massive assembly and waste reduction projects functioned smoothly under Henry Ford's leadership and care. His death in 1947 started the decline of this great complex, which would reflect the very history of America's industrial gains and losses.

Ford's son, Henry Ford II, was more than happy to change the direction of the Rouge to a modern bureaucratic factory, paying less attention to the endless details required for recycling and waste reduction. In fact, the new managers saw recycling, agricultural plastics, the sale of by-products, and alcohol car fuel as a cost stream in the abundance of the 1950s. The transition of Ford Motor from Henry Ford to his son marked the end of paternal capitalism at the Rouge, and the passion was gone. Henry Ford's passion had made up for any inefficiency of his concepts. The torch of the Rouge's innovative manufacturing would be passed to Toyota, who admired this great plant.

Just before Ford retired, Mr. Toyota and his engineers spent 6 months in 1946 at the Rouge, studying Ford's methods. Toyota built on Ford's concepts to develop the company's now famous "lean manufacture" based on waste elimination. He found few American companies open to a long term visit. Ford, a believer in world peace, was happy to share his ideas — now being rejected by his new managers — with a Toyota who idealized him. What they saw was not the powerful assembly methodology, but the synergy in the company of waste elimination. Company owner Toyota Toyoda and Toyota Company would take the torch of Ford's lean philosophy and create the world's most profitable auto company in Japan. Today, American industry is returning to Ford's original philosophy through Toyota's leadership.

Toyota and the Japanese automakers have roots going back to the early 1930s with a government push for national industrialization. Toyota and Datsun took the lead in the effort to break the American car monopoly. World War II caused Japanese automakers to focus on truck production. After the war, Toyota was given permission by the United States to resume auto production. The depressed domestic market and limited manufacturing capacity required a far different approach to manufacture than that used in the United States. The very weakness of their auto industry would, in the long run, become the basis of its strength today. The total monthly production of Toyota was around 10,000 units, or roughly a day's production of one American auto plant. In addition, Toyota had to produce all kinds of products such as trucks, car, taxis, and fire engines. The market and limited capacity resulted in much more flexible approach to manufacturing, which can be seen today in lean manufacture. Toyota saw at the Rouge a concept of a supplier city for a central assembly line. Such an arrangement would give Toyota the methodology to make quick model changes on an assembly. Ford would have done this in the 1940s, but demand focused him on one model assembly. While American assembly lines focused on economies of scale from volume, Japanese assembly lines focused on product flexibility, rapid tooling change, efficiency, and continuous cost cutting. The company maintained an aggressive vision of becoming an international manufacturer even in these early days.

In America, many expected a more centralized and fast paced automation for the future. The Rouge, after Ford's death, however, followed a path of decentralization. The new whiz kid managers of Henry Ford II applied new cost accounting methodology, which made the original self-sufficient integrated approach look unprofitable. Ford's concept of "ore to assembly" was dumped and replaced with supply chain decentralization. In 1981, the steel operations would become an independent company and much of the ore handling operations were sold. In 1992, the plant was producing only the Ford Mustang and was facing permanent closure. The union and community rallied and actually created a surge in Mustang sales.

The Rouge plant was saved by a special agreement with the United Auto Workers that moved the plant into the new millennium. Known as the "Rouge Viability Agreement," it created a flexible manufacturing center in 1998. Today the Rouge employs 6,000 employees, making it Ford's largest plant. It is highly flexible and efficient, building nine models on three different platforms. The plant has returned to its early environmental and recycling focus and is a showcase of auto manufacturing for the future. The steel plant remains in place; it is currently owned by a Russian steelmaker — Severstal North America. Many of the paternal management methods of Henry Ford have returned. The Rouge offers hope despite the bad news of globalization and de-industrialization. The study of Henry Ford's early strategy offers a back-to-the-future path.[1]

America would build one last iconic assembly plant before de-industrialization: the robotic monster of General Motors at Lordstown, Ohio. Lordstown was the heart of industrial America, with the rubber compa-

---

1 Quentin Skrabec, *The Green Vision of Henry Ford and George Washington Carver: Two Collaborators in the Cause of a Clean and Green Industry*, (Jefferson: McFarland, 2013), p. 25

nies of Akron and steel of Youngstown and Pittsburgh within 60 miles. The mile-long plant was built in 1966 for a cost of 100 million dollars. Maybe more impressive was that 900 small companies within the 60 mile radius were supplying goods and services to Lordstown. Lordstown and the Rouge illustrate a little quoted fact — while small business creates more jobs than big business, big business is the biggest creator of small business. Lordstown, like the Rouge, remains a local anchor for jobs.

Originally designed to produce 60 cars per hour, the Lordstown plant was re-tooled in 1970 to build the Vega at a rate of 100 cars per hour. This was by far the fastest assembly in the world in 1970. The Vega was a sub-compact meant to meet the Japanese competition head-on before even the oil crisis of the 1970s. The 1970 retooling reduced the time a worker had to do his job from a minute to 36 seconds. One shift started to hit an amazing rate of 110-cars per minute, but this proved to be unsustainable. The 100-car rate for the individual worker proved to be the ultimate worker/machine barrier. More importantly, as the workers moved past the one-minute-per-operation barrier, the human machine broke down. Automation had gotten ahead of the worker, and industry had also gotten ahead of the community.

Lordstown, even more than the transition at Ford, marked the end of paternal capitalism in American industry. Paternal capitalism, despite all the criticism, still had a passion for industrial growth, a connection to community and country, and a heart. The new managers of the 1960s were university-trained and mobile. Community factored little in their business decisions. They saw the need for efficiency and productivity in global competition. What they didn't see was the role of the worker or community in that effort. Accounting, robotics, and productivity goals were all that was needed. The lack of heart and even passion was reflected in the low motivation of the workers.

Lordstown would soon become a center of union resistance and neo-Luddite activity. The neo-Luddites, being reminiscent of the famous Luddites of England in 1812 who took to destroying the automatic looms of the new factories. The Luddites represented the first resistance to the fast paced systems and job loss of the Industrial Revolution. Lordstown should have been America's way forward for global competition; but unlike Henry Ford, who spent as much in the design of human systems to match his mechanical assembly, managers at Lordstown ignored the human/machine interface. The pace created absenteeism and tardiness rates over 20 percent, and the local union resisted the line pace. Quality dropped off, making the Vega uncompetitive against the high targeted quality of Japanese competition.

Henry Ford had found the same resistance with the implementation of his first assembly line production. Ford bought time for the workers to adjust by doubling their pay in the 1920s to an amazing $5.00 a day. General Motors, in a competitive squeeze, didn't have that option at Lordstown. Management stood steady but the workers adjusted with a type of sabotage of production. Often bolts, nuts, and engine parts were left out.[1] Sales started to be affected as the media picked up on the story. The cost estimated by General Motors had hit $45 million, and 900 employees were disciplined for their role in sabotage.[2] The trouble led to a 22-day strike, during which the United Auto Workers won most of their points.

Sadly, Lordstown was a loss for American manufacturing overall. What might have been a model for slowing the onrush of imports that was soon unleashed in the 1973 Oil Crisis, became a major setback. Fifteen years later, the *Los Angeles Times* saw it in generational terms of a relatively wealthy baby boomer class. The description was a powerful statement: "The labor–management war at Lordstown was widely viewed as a direct challenge to the established industrial order in America, the blue-collar equivalent of the anti-war demonstrations then being mounted by college students against the nation's political establishment. . . With young, long haired workers flashing the peace sign at reporters, the Lordstown turmoil was soon being described as an industrial Woodstock. . . perhaps for the first time, the factory workers of the baby boom generation would not put up with the same conditions that their fathers and grandfathers had so readily accepted in return for a paycheck."[3] Not surprisingly, the political epicenter of the Vietnam War protests was located twenty miles down the road in 1970 with the Kent State National Guard shootings.

Lordstown, more than any other auto plant, was manned by baby boomers. These boomers didn't trust business or government, but they expected to earn a good living. In retrospect, it was a time of economic plenty, and few foresaw the collapse on the horizon. The booming steel, rubber, and auto production of the Lordstown region was soon to become the heart of America's rustbelt. Still, Lordstown did not collapse with the Chevy Vega. Vega had gone too far in technology for smooth production at a labor troubled plant. Lordstown was re-tooled in the late 1970s

---

1 *Cleveland Plain Dealer*, January 23, 1972
2 *Cleveland Plain Dealer*, February 7, 1972
3 James Risen, "Truce in Labor War," *Los Angeles Times*, June 10, 1987

for J cars (the best known was the Cavalier). General Motors hoped that the Lordstown-built Cavalier could take on Japanese imports. But for General Motors to win the battle of the small cars, they needed the productivity levels proposed for the Lordstown plant to offset the high labor costs. Estimates were that the Japanese had a $1,000 to $2,000 cost advantage. About $500 was accounted for by lower Japanese wages with the balance being productivity advantages. The Japanese used 50 percent less labor hours per car.

Lordstown's automated assembly was equal to, if not superior to, the Japanese; but Japanese had followed the plant design that they learned from Henry Ford. They better understood the coordination of humans and machines. They also had better integration of suppliers based on the early work of Henry Ford. Their plants, like the Rouge, were fully integrated with supplier cities surrounding plants. Lordstown brought subassemblies in from thousands of locations. Engines, for example, came from plants in Flint, Michigan, and Tonawanda, New York. Transmissions came from Ypsilanti, Michigan, power steering from Saginaw, Michigan, and engine mounts from Dayton, Ohio. One of the top automotive journalists of the time summarized it this way: "Accumulating an inventory of parts from all over the country, even overseas, was a nightmarish task involving a vast transportation and warehousing operation that placed GM at distinct disadvantage with the Japanese. . . The Lordstown facility had to keep a ten-day supply of components on hand, which entailed added costs in handling and storage. 'Some of the parts are handled up to thirty-two times before they actually end up on the automobile.'[1]

General Motors management was not as dumb as they are often presented in giving reasons for de-industrialization. While it was too late to adapt at Lordstown, the Buick Division of General Motors moved to a "supplier city" concept at its Flint, Michigan plant in 1982. The idea was to have the suppliers locate their plants at the assembly plant. Again, it was the very design of Henry Ford's Rouge plant in the 1920s. Buick City did take on the Japanese, but it was too little too late. The Buick City plant was feeding light trucks into a market that for General Motors was declining; they were being driven out by cheaper Japanese trucks. By 1999, Buick City, the last assembly plant in Flint, was closed as part of a broader reorganization.

---

1 Brock Yates, *The Decline & Fall of the American Automobile Industry*, (New York: Vintage Books, 1984), p. 56

The Japanese use of Ford process integration created a marketing revolution in America as well. The Japanese's long distribution network was a weakness that became a strength. Many auto insiders believed that the Chevy Cavalier could have competed head on with the Japanese if it was not for the marketing strategy of loading options on base models. The Japanese, with a 6,000 mile pipeline, were forced to sell a basic car with few options. Honda, in particular, had a car for less than $7,000 on the market in 1982. The Cavalier had a base price of $6,549, but to add the options consumers had come to expect and Honda delivered, such as air conditioning ($625), power steering ($199), and cassette player ($455), took the car over $10,000. The Cavalier continued production problems at Lordstown, and Chevy's marketing put the car with the earlier small car failures of Corvair and Vega.

Lordstown and the Rouge represented two phases of the American Industrial Revolution. Conneaut represented the industrial future that was never to be. Maybe Conneaut was the greatest factory of the American experience that was never built; for four generations it had been an industrial dream. Conneaut was the super mill that Andrew Carnegie announced in 1901. He had been planning it for years, to fully integrate and automate steelmaking; but the merger to form United States Steel put it on the back burner. It was to be Carnegie's steel version of Henry Ford's Rouge. The plan was dusted off in the 1970s, since United States Steel still owned the deep water port of Conneaut on Lake Erie. Steel mills, even into the 1970s, were notoriously inefficient and energy wasteful. They were monuments to a world of plenty and little competition. Mills often cooled and reheated steel to thousands of degrees a number of times as each operation might take place in a different location, requiring more internal transportation. Handling costs were as high as 70 percent of the manufacturing costs of steel. The Conneaut plant, never built, would have been the most efficient steel plant in the world, but in the real world these US mills, while productive, were not capable of competing in the post-war world.

The "Millionaire's Dinner" that marked the formation of United States Steel on January 9, 1901, at Pittsburgh's Hotel Schenley, was meant to include the announcement of Carnegie's Conneaut super mill. This dinner assembled over 89 millionaires in one room, something that had never occurred in the history of the world. These millionaires were the result of Carnegie partners being paid for their shares. Charles Schwab had planned the great celebration a year after the end of the Carnegie partnership which created these 89 millionaires. Schwab was becoming quite a party boy now. He had set the theme of the great dinner to be "Expectations." The future looked even brighter because Carnegie Steel had announced plans to invest $12 million in the world's largest steel tube mill to be built at Conneaut, Ohio. The Conneaut mill was a direct challenge to the newly formed "Chicago Steel Trust" of J.P. Morgan. Conneaut was to be a super mill of fully-integrated operations unequalled in the world. It would be built at the deep water port of Conneaut, Ohio, to automatically unload ore from the Great Lakes.

In 1896, Andrew Carnegie had improved the deep water port at Conneaut by founding the Pittsburgh & Conneaut Dock Company. Unable to make arrangements with the Pennsylvania Railroad, Carnegie built his own railroad, the Pittsburgh, Shenango, and Lake Erie Railroad, to bring 2,000,000 tons of iron ore to his Pittsburgh mills. But the formation of United States Steel in 1901 changed everything. The company was no longer run by steelmakers, but the bankers of J.P. Morgan. Old Carnegie steel men like Charles Schwab would fight for years for the Conneaut super mill, only to be turned out of the company in the 1920s. While United States Steel would always have a rebel pocket of old Carnegie steel managers, the bankers were fully in control.

The great vision of an integrated mill at Conneaut re-surfaced in the 1970s. United States Steel had owned the virgin site since the Carnegie purchase in 1896. One of the old Carnegie-style managers, Edgar Speer, dusted off the old dream of Conneaut. On Speer's rise to CEO of United States Steel, it was said that "no one in the world knew more about steel production... after twenty-three years in the works, Speer brought to his tenure at the top post a "romantic" attachment to the big steel image of the past."[1] He was a man out of the mold of Carnegie and Charles Schwab, but he would find the same resistance of the Morgan bankers. Still, Speer might have pulled it off if the 1975 steel recession had not struck in the midst of a flood of steel and auto imports.

From 1973 to 1977, steel imports jumped 50 percent, eliminating the belief that USS needed more steel capacity. Another nail in the coffin came with the new environmental regulations of the Carver Administration which would have doubled the cost of building. The Conneaut investment "was shunned on the basis of purely accounting considerations. The accountant's mentality that prevails at US Steel dictated that new investments would have to yield a high enough return to maintain

---

1 Kenneth Warren, *Big Steel: The First Century of United States Corporation*, (Pittsburgh: University of Pittsburgh Press, 2003), p. 305

the going rate of return."[1] In a related press conference in 1977, a USS executive said "We Make Profits, Not Steel," to which a reporter noted, "Andrew Carnegie would turn over in his grave if he heard that."[2] Conneaut remained on the drawing boards through the 1980s but was never built. De-industrialization stripped available capital from United States Steel. Big banks were also financing the Japanese steel expansion and profiting from imports into the United States during the same time period. Conneaut is illustrative of a larger problem in America's approach to early de-industrialization.

Great industrialists such as Andrew Carnegie and Henry Ford were gone. Banking executives ran America's industries by the 1970s. MBA-trained managers saw profits and globalization as the Golden Fleece. United States Steel's purchase of Marathon Oil in 1981 was an example of making profits over steel. Bankers like J.P. Morgan had always been around, but men like Carnegie, Ford, Firestone, Schwab, Westinghouse, and Heinz had opposed inference in operations by bankers. Ford and Westinghouse had even been vocal, decrying the end of American industry, should bankers take control. Furthermore, the operations managers so sought and trained by these industrial founders were now replaced with a new breed of accounting and financial based managers. It was said that in postwar America corporations were no longer people but the stock certificates held by the bank. The goal of capitalism shifted from making things to gaining return on investment. Not surprisingly, by 1980, Japan made 16 percent of the world's steel to the falling 14 percent made by the United States. The American government and businesses (and maybe in the case of the Lordstown workers as well) were not interested in being the world's manufacturer, preferring to be its banker.

Many have decried the shift in top management from operations backgrounds to financial backgrounds as a root cause of de-industrialization. Certainly such a shift was seen in the auto, steel, and rubber industries. It was exactly what the old lions feared. Still, the shift to financial executives came with a great struggle internally. For companies like Firestone and United States Steel, the old lions gave sometimes heroic fights to retain the factories and plants. It was de-industrialization itself that brought on this shift in top management as it paralleled the shift from national and paternal capitalism to international capitalism.

1 Lydia Dittler, "U. S. Steel Corp: We Make Profits, Not Steel," *Executive Intelligence Review*, Vol. 4 Number 50, December 13, 1977
2 Ibid.

Lordstown, the Rouge, and the failed hope of Conneaut were repeated across the US on a lesser scale throughout the early twentieth century but faded by the 1970s. The paternal and national capitalism of men like Andrew Carnegie and Henry Ford that had given these towns their great factories had died. Workers, businessmen, communities, and even the government seemed no longer to want this type of capitalism. Prosperity had masked its benefits and made big business and the unions look like the enemy. Cities became divided instead of united. Teachers and government workers unionized. Well-paid industrial workers, their basic needs covered, looked to higher needs, taking the basic needs for granted. Prosperity in the initial stages of de-industrialization left many workers unemployed as they would not settle for lower pay or step up to meet a faster work pace. De-industrialization took hold during the era of the baby boomers who had never known hard times. Paternal capitalism seemed like unneeded welfare capitalism, more patronizing than paternal. These baby boomers simply took for granted good pay and benefits from big business, and outstanding social services.

Maybe a better term for this old-style American capitalism is the one used by social historian John Cumbler — civic capitalism. Civic capitalism grew out of the earlier paternal capitalism but expanded to even small business. Small businesses supported scouts, baseball teams, parks, and other civic projects. Feudal as capitalism appeared in the 1960s, it was the fiber of most American cities. Cities were known for what they made or what products were made there. In years of prosperity, people lost sight of the role of civic capitalism in supporting social services, schools, community events, churches, and lowering crime. Today's international capitalism of trade and banking does little for the cities and workers. International capitalism favored big international businesses, moving far from the medieval town markets in Germany. But international capitalism assured the de-industrialization of America.

Chapter 6. And the Wolf Finally Came — the 1970s

The later part of the 1970s saw the appearance of the Four Horsemen in the American economy of de-industrialization. Free trade imports, aging plants and assets, global labor competition, and rapid technological change came to devastate American industry. These plagues had not been fully foreseen at the Mont Pèlerin conference of 1947.

The later part of the 1970s saw a loss of 32 million industrial jobs.[1] America's great cities of the industrial age were in decline. De-industrialization did do more than change geography books. It would change social norms and old immigrant infrastructure in many of those industrial cities such as Detroit, Cleveland, Pittsburgh, Youngstown, Akron, Buffalo, Trenton, Philadelphia, Newark, Cincinnati, St. Louis, Chicago and many others. Smaller industrial towns across the nation would be returned to pre-industrial days. Families and neighborhoods changed with the loss of industrial plants and social norms did too. Family and community safety networks disappeared, requiring government to step in. De-industrialization fundamentally changed society.

The automotive, steel, rubber, and textile industries stumbled first, but the trend would spread through all of American industries. The first horseman of the industrial apocalypse would be an import, such as autos, rubber tires, and steel. The second was the competiveness of these imports because of foreign labor was paid less so the manufactur-

---

1 Barry Bluestone and Bennett Harrison, *The Deindustrialization of America*, (New York: Basic Books, 1982), p. 37

ing costs were less. The third horseman was the modern factories of a restored Europe and Japan; they overwhelmed America's aging factories of the World War II. The final crushing blow was new foreign technology such as French steel-belted radial tires and mini-steel mill electric furnace technology. In the late 1970s these horsemen converged.

Imports led that charge. Imports represented both a symptom and a problem of de-industrialization. By the 1970s management inadequacies, aging plants, over-demanding unions, and government policies all left American industry vulnerable to the appeal of imports, and this all resulted in the collapse of American manufacturing over the next 50 years. The arrival of the first Japanese imported car in 1957 was a sign, but was not clear enough to provoke an epiphany for America. America seemed invincible in 1957 with four out five cars in the world being built in the United States. "Made in America" was a stamp of quality. A domestic manufactured car in 1957 was 100 percent American parts. Industrial America bought American, and that was its armor. The chink in the industrial armor was found in the steel industry.

At its 1940s peak America made over 60 percent of the world's steel. The real turning point was the Steel Strike of 1959. The three-month 1959 Strike changed America's attitude about imports. Auto manufacturers and others were forced to buy imported steel, and they soon realized the benefits of cheaper, high-quality steel from the rebuilt mills of Europe and Japan. That strike cost American steel a huge loss of market that never returned. Overseas steel quickly established a supply network. Furthermore, this set the stage for the 1960s which saw imported steel reach near 20 percent in the early 1970s.

Now the flood gates were opened to steel imports. After the 1959 strike, US steel production was at 26 percent of the total world market (the lowest since the 1870s). Prior to the Strike, steel prosperity in the early 1950s had enabled the unions to negotiate favorable contracts. In 1956, the United Steelworkers had won large wage increases of four to six percent per year. In 1959, American steelworkers were earning $2.92 an hour compared to 75 cents an hour in Germany and 45 cents an hour in Japan. Japan mills were now modernized and producing world class steel at low prices thanks to American and Japanese banks which had backed the modernization.

Many critics still say that the American steel industry was not investing in plant modernization, but the facts are much different. The first response of the United States, under the Kennedy Administration, was to simulate investment in rebuilding old mills. In 1962, a Revenue Act offered steel companies and others tax credits for plant investment. This was a highly successful tax policy. The steel industry responded with over $16 billion of modernization, a 50 percent increase over the decade of the 1950s. The industry not only modernized but over expanded to fight the flood of imports after the 1959 strike. The issue was that Japan and Europe wanted to expand their steel industry and backed the expansion with trade and financial incentives to offset any American modernization; and America continued to hold to the newly adopted economic philosophy of the Mont Pèlerin Society, promoting free trade (duty free).

There were few actual examples of the widely held myth that businesses were failing to invest in modernization in the late 1970s; but to a large degree, the game was already over, and heavy industry correctly looked to get a better return on their shrinking dollars.

The final economic boom in steel came in 1970 and it masked the real structural problems. In 1968, the steel industry and the steel unions had been lulled by a voluntary agreement with friendly nations not to dump steel. The arrangement actually was successful until the steel boom in 1970, which saw temporary steel shortages and price increases. In 1971, Congress let the voluntary agreement expire. The year 1972 would be the steel industry's last hurrah; steel shipments started to fall rapidly, including raw steel imports, steel parts imports, capital goods imports, and automobile imports. The boom was a memory by 1975, as American steel realized it might be too late to return to its glory days.

The boom-bust cycle of the 1970s masked the real problem, and religious adherence to free-trade policies of the "Austrian School" was to blame. That economic theory was the single most devastating import. Sadly, de-industrialization in America was a result of a nation turned against itself. The philosophy of the automotive industry supply chain became "save yourself." De-industrialization came in waves by industry and region. The steel and rubber industries were hit hard in the 1970s. Part of the problem was the industrial supply chain turned on itself for survival. In the late 1960s, the steel industry mounted a cry for help, asking Congress for tariffs on imported steel which had gone from 1.1 million tons in 1957 to 17.9 million tons in 1968. Steel users now being supplied with cheap imported steel were willing to sacrifice the American steel industry to save their own industries.

Congress might have stopped the dumping of steel if it had not been for powerful bankers and steel users opposing tariffs. This powerful opposition against tariffs was known as the "Emergency Committee for American Trade." This group held up the flag of free trade, and the ongoing international movement of the Mont Pèlerin Society — known as the World Trade Organization — threw domestic steel to the sharks. It was hard for Congress to find an economist at any big-name university to seriously advocate protectionism. Banks had also loaded up with young Hayek-inspired economists on the "Emergency Committee." In fact, Hayek, the founder of the Mont Pèlerin Society, declared in 1978, "As far as the movement of intellectual opinion is concerned, it is now the first time in my life things are moving in the right direction."[1]

The "Emergency Committee" was led by the banking CEOs of Lehman Brothers, Bank of America, First National City, and Chase Manhattan. The banks profited the most from open free trade. More disappointing was the major American steel users who wanted to improve their own competitiveness, such as General Motors, Ford, Caterpillar Tractor, Deere & Company, and Heinz. This would have appalled the patriotic capitalists that founded these companies. The "Emergency Committee" would win by making believe that capitalism and free trade were one and the same thing.

More importantly, they won over conservative Republicans who for over hundred years had been the buttress protecting American industry. It was in vogue to label anti-free traders as anti-American capitalism. Liberal Democrats were won over by university "Austrian School" economists who warned of trade wars and a return to a 1930s-style depression if tariffs were put in place. Free-trade economists had raised fear of trade wars to the level of the fear of a nuclear attack in 1950s. This trade war fear of liberals and conservatives would, to a large degree, take de-industrialization out of the debate. Congress would instead focus on social and unemployment benefits for displaced workers.

Interestingly, the auto companies would come begging to Congress decades later for help against imports. This, however, has been the nature of de-industrialization (slow, industry by industry). De-industrialization played on the well-known weaknesses of capitalism — greed and self-interest. The auto and capital goods supply chains and their related political networks turned to self-preservation versus the national interest. Gone was the patriotic and nationalistic capitalism of America's industrial founders.

In the later years of the 1970s, twenty-five auto plants would close — thirteen Chrysler plants, seven General Motors, and five Ford plants. These closings would oust over 500,000 workers in the auto industry and

1 Nicholas Wapshott, *Keynes Hayek: The Clash That Defined Modern Economics*, (New York: W. W. Norton & Company, 2011), p. 268

supply chain. Not only did the slump in the auto industry hit the steel and rubber industries, but both came under the direct attack of foreign competition as well. The job losses were, of course, much greater. One continual urban legend is that small business creates most of America's jobs, which is true. Big business wages are the generators that drive small business. Any citizen of a town with a large factory soon learns this as pizza shops, lawn services, restaurants, and whole strip malls close soon after the factory does. The more mobile professionals such as dentists, doctors, and optometrists leave town, too.

Thanksgiving Day 1979 was another mile marker. During 1979, the auto industry announced the imminent shutdown of twenty plants, affecting 50,000 autoworkers and another 300,000 in the auto supply chain. November in the city of Pittsburgh started as a great party with the Pittsburgh Pirates, having just won the World Series, and the Pittsburgh Steelers on their way to a second Super Bowl win. Billboards outside the city's steel mills hailed the "City of Champions." Employees of United States Steel faced a more sober reality. The Thanksgiving message from United States Steel was the closing of 14 mills around the country. Pittsburgh's Mon Valley (along the Monongahela River) would be hit hard, but it would be a death knell for nearby Youngstown, Ohio.

Two years earlier Youngstown had lost its iconic Campbell Works of Youngstown Sheet & Tube. Youngstown Sheet & Tube neared bankruptcy in the late 1970s, and the huge settlement with the union in 1977 forced them to sell assets. The Youngstown area had mills from six steelmakers, but they were old mills and were losing customers to the new postwar mills of the world. LTV Steel took over the old Sheet & Tube mills in 1978, but it was short-lived relief. Most realized that with Thanksgiving of 1979, the steel glory days of Youngstown were over for good.

The talk at Thanksgiving tables 40 miles away in Akron, Ohio, was no better. For the last two years, Firestone, Goodyear, Goodrich, and Mohawk had closed down major rubber-making plants in Akron. In all, Akron would lose an amazing 30,000 rubber jobs in the 1970s. Their old plants equipped only to make old-fashioned bias-ply tire were unable to compete with radial tires from France (Michelin) and radials from Japan (Bridgestone). The conversion to radial technology required the gutting of old plant equipment and huge capital investment. Like steel, the fall of rubber went beyond the "Rubber City." In the last 5 years of the 1970s, 24 rubber plants closed, with 11 of them being in the South. It was the one-two punch of radial technology and auto imports.

De-industrialization struck many industries in 1979. Unemployed workers from Westinghouse Electric and Stauffer Chemical in New Jersey, Weyerhaeuser timber mills on the West Coast, and textile workers in North Carolina gathered for Thanksgiving dinner with the same concerns as families in Youngstown and Pittsburgh. And it wasn't just rust-belt and Southern cities. Los Angeles lost eight major factories including Ford Motor, US Steel, Uniroyal, Pabst Beer, and General Electric in 1979 with 18,000 people losing their jobs. By early 1980, over 150 plants in California closed. De-industrialization struck with such speed that the local politicians were unable to coordinate a response. A little too late, congressmen in many states realized the national importance of industries such as steel. But the outcry to "protect our industries" was drowned out by the rising popularity of free trade economics in both parties.

The West would feel the imports first in all the major industries. The rubber industry collapse was far-reaching including the three iconic Los Angeles plants of Goodyear, Goodrich, and Firestone that brought tire making to America's West Coast. The Goodyear's Los Angeles plant had been the first tire plant built outside of Akron, in 1919. It closed in 1975. Now the West Coast was rolled by a tsunami of imported Japanese radial tires. Interestingly, Los Angeles had been the center from which the American tire companies had expanded internationally in the 1920s and 1930s. The United States Steel plant at Pittsburgh went bankrupt, and Kaiser Steel,

a bit east of Los Angeles would follow in bankruptcy.

America, as a whole, accepted the de-industrialization stoically. Economic change that over the last two hundred years had created revolution and political upheaval in Europe came to America with no street protests. Americans were by nature optimistic and saw de-industrialization as temporary and painful like that of the 1930s. Economists said it was part of globalization and new opportunities would arise. Many talked of America being in a "post-industrial" era of information and high tech industries. The government poured money into retraining programs for displaced workers. Academics even called it creative destruction as a natural part of the shift from manual to mental work. Blame was passed around to unions, management, banks, Wall Street, one political party or the other, and, of course, imports. Political solutions went to the symptoms. Huge amounts of federal money were injected in retraining. Government safety nets and union protections were added to lessen the losses. The economy, to some degree, absorbed the younger industrial workers into lower paying jobs in retailing and small business. The initial heavy impact on blue collar workers made the popular solution a college degree, and community colleges were a growth area.

Industrial America adjusted in the 1970s. Income was lost and reduced American families to two incomes. In many industrial neighborhoods, this change from a head of the household one income created major social changes. Many of these neighborhoods in cities such as Cleveland and Pittsburgh had the social infrastructure of the 1890s and had seen little change until the 1970s. The American industrial worker absorbed the shock of de-industrialization in the 1970s. Part of that flexibility was the ability to maintain high family incomes through two income families. The older industrial cities tended to follow their immigrant roots in having a head of the household income. The 1970s saw a shift, particularly with younger couples, to a two income family. Family size was also adjusted downward to maintain standard of living. Some of the change was already underway in the late 1960s, but the loss of high paying jobs made it a necessity for many.

Geo-social changes were just as dramatic. Once large cities such as Pittsburgh, Buffalo, St. Louis, and Cleveland fell down, the population rankings of Southern cities like Houston rocketed up. The northern industrial cities saw their own decline with the loss of business, sales, and individual taxes. Florida grew also as big industries used buyouts to lower operating wages by forcing retirements. In older steel companies like Republic Steel, 50-year-old workers with 30 years or more could retire with a cash bonus between $250,000 to $500,000 or a lifetime of inequity payments. Many headed to Florida and formed company retirement clubs. For some major company policies, operation managers would often make presentations to these retirement clubs because of their political power in company politics. While early retirement offers helped to reduce current operating cost, it only added to the legacy costs of retirement payments. LTV Steel had so aggressively forced early retirement that by 1984, the company had six retirees on the rolls for every active employee. Large industrial companies had become social welfare organizations versus profit producing companies. Iconic industrial areas would become pockets of crime and homeless.

Chapter 7. Youngstown and the Mahoning Valley Falls

Youngstown, Ohio, was steel. It was more dependent on steel than Pittsburgh. It had blast furnaces before Pittsburgh. The Mahoning Valley included the steel mills of Youngstown, Niles, and Warren along a 25 mile stretch. The mill closings of Youngstown Sheet & Tube, United States Steel, Sharon Steel, Copperweld, and Republic Steel from 1977 to the mid-1980s resulted in the loss of an estimated 40,000 jobs. Small businesses collapsed throughout the valley and school taxes losses destroyed the city system. By 1995, Youngtown looked like Germany at the end of World War II. The social and community infrastructure collapsed as crime took over the valley. It would auger the future of many rustbelt cities. The dynamiting of the three great blast furnaces of United States Steel Ohio Works on August 7, 1984 would be an iconic picture that ran in the world's newspapers.

Bruce Springsteen released his song 'Youngstown" in 1995 that covered the pain of 50,000 steelworkers who had lost their jobs. Not surprisingly, for in Bruce Springsteen's youth, many of these workers vacationed in his home state of New Jersey at the shore. Few realized that "my sweet Jenny" in the song was not a woman but the famous Jeanette blast furnace of Youngstown Sheet and Tube's Brier Hill mill. Blast furnaces in the United States were always named after women. Jenny was named after the president of Brier Hill Steel's daughter in 1918. Jenny, while no longer making iron but still standing at the time of the song, would fall, to the tears of many, in 1997. Jenny had supplied iron to make steel using 10,000 workers in the process. The Brier Hill area of Youngstown was a total steel neighborhood. The huge coal deposit of Brier Hill had been the source of steelmaking coming to Mahoning Valley in the 1800s. Brier Hill was a community of five generations of steel workers. Even the frieze on the town's St. Anthony Church depicted St. Joseph helping a steelworker shove coal into a steel furnace. Nearby Our Lady of Mount Carmel Church showed St. Joseph making hot steel, and St. John Episcopal had a stained glass window representing steel management and collective bargaining.

Not surprisingly, it was a coalition of church organizations that led the fight to save the Youngtown steel mills. That coalition made a mark on de-industrialization, challenging the logic of Mont Pèlerin: "They challenged the notion that shutdowns were part of natural economic order, and they reminded a nation of the social and moral dimensions of de-industrialization."[1] While Youngstown failed locally, it was able to move Congress to enact legislation requiring community notifications of massive pull outs, and it established a principle of community eminent domain over private industrial property to be returned to the community. These, however, were small victories, which did not address the core cause.

The Youngstown area was proud and happy of what Springsteen described as the "beautiful sky of soot and clay." Such a love may seem strange to those who have lived in the country, but it's a love that ran deep. Under the dirt and pollution, there was a vibrant culture. Local historians described it this way: "For many years the area had a clear sense of itself as one of the most important industrial communities in the United States. Youngstowners were proud not only of what they produced, but also of the benefits brought by their efforts — high rates of home ownership, impressive cultural resources, and a deep sense of home loyalty. At the same time, especially among Youngstown's working class, the community took pride in its history as a site of struggle for workers' rights."[2] It may seem strange that the inhabitants of these dirty, smoky steel towns had access (often free) to the world's greatest libraries, art museums, cultural centers, parks designed by the world best architects, and educational institutes. Generations would continue to reap the rewards of these libraries and museums.

1 Sherry Lee Linkon and John Russo, *Steel-Town U.S.A.*, (Lawrence: University of Kansas Press, 2002), p. 50
2 Sherry Lee Linkon and John Russo, *Steel-Town U.S.A.*, (Lawrence: University of Kansas Press, 2002), p. 2

Youngstown had blast furnaces and was making steel before Pittsburgh. In fact, Youngstown would have 11 blast furnaces in the valley before Pittsburgh got its first. The area was driven by the rich coal segments on Brier Hill in the 1840s. Small charcoal furnaces, which had made cannonballs for the War of 1812, were converted to coal by 1846. The canal connections came to Youngstown in the 1850s which could bring iron ore from Michigan and more coal from Southern Ohio, and ship raw pig iron to be processed in Pittsburgh's rolling mills. In 1859, Brier Hill Steel was a leader in the industry with the world's largest blast furnaces. Brier Hill Steel would morph into Youngstown Sheet & Tube in 1912. By 1918, United States Steel had Campbell Works, and Republic Steel had a plant in Warren. Youngstown stood second to Pittsburgh in steel production and was often compared to Germany's Ruhr Valley.

The region (Niles) had given birth to William McKinley whose protectionist policies had given birth to the nation's steel industry. The McKinley family had been one of the area's first steelmakers. It was well remembered that when the funeral train of the assassinated President McKinley in 1901 came slowly through Pittsburgh and Youngtown, thousands of steel workers held up their dinner pails as a tribute to McKinley. The now forgotten McKinley Presidential Memorial in Niles had been a gift of the nation's greatest iron and steel men. The library remains a bronze pantheon of busts of these great steelmakers and a tribute to the steel industry. It is said that it was the only place where the stoic, emotionless steel titan, Henry Clay Frick, cried at the end of his life lamenting the glory days of Carnegie Steel. Today, this location represents the beginning of the end of the American steel industry.

The pressure of imports in the 1960s and 1970s put Youngstown in a tough position. Its steel furnaces were of the older open hearth type, which were far less productive than the Basic Oxygen Furnace. It put the Youngstown mills at a distinct disadvantage even against other domestic competitors. The pressure mounted to increase output and productivity. This would lead to a decline in quality to meet competitive output goals. The year 1977 saw the steel market fall into shambles as imported steel poured in at $100 a ton below domestic prices. Even major reduction in labor costs would not have closed the price difference. Japan was producing steel well over its domestic needs and was a world supplier. Furthermore, the share size of Japan's over expanded production required it to work at high capacity (70 percent) to stay efficient.[1]

---

1 William T. Hogan, *World Steel in the 1980s*, (Lexington: Lexington Books, 1983), p. 208

Europe was also hit by a flood of imports, but many decided to nationalize the steel industry because it was a major employer. America was philosophically stuck between in a political framework that opposed tariffs, wanted a high dollar (making American steel more costly), opposed nationalization, and wanted to promote world trade. It was a deadly combination that would only result in the de-industrialization of America. The flood of imports would now break the back of America's weakest producers. What has become known as "Black Monday," September 19, 1977, was not only the death knell of Youngstown Sheet & Tube Steel but the beginning of the end of American steel.

Youngstown reflects another part of de-industrialization, that of community identity. Local historians, Sherry Lee Linkon and John Russo, described it as, "When mills began to close in the late 1970s, the core of community and individual identity shifted, and the meaning of Youngstown and the meaning of work in Youngstown would first be transformed and then deformed. Once a site of productive labor and class struggle, Youngstown would become a place known for economic loss and resistance. The struggle in Youngstown would not end in the closing of the mill."[1] This communal grief would be seen in other cities as well such as Akron, Detroit, Toledo, Pittsburgh, Trenton, Buffalo, and many smaller towns. The phases of this communal grief are amazingly similar to that of individuals.

Youngstown first experienced disbelief, which made things worse in trying to save a smaller portion of the steel industry. This was followed by communal bargaining from the unions and churches to gain government help to save the industry. Failures in these efforts lead to a need to honor the heritage of Youngstown. Youngstown Area Arts Council hired George Segal to create a huge sculpture of steelmaking in the heart of the city. These life size bronze statues of steelworkers tending an open-hearth furnace were striking. The open-hearth furnace was, to many, an older technology that had doomed Youngstown. Artwork, poems, and photos of the old steel making days flooded the Butler Institute of Art in Youngstown. Steel magnate Joe Butler was the Andrew Carnegie of Youngstown and his art museum was a symbol of the city's glory. It was a struggle for a city to leave its steel making heritage behind. This struggle to accept de-industrialization by first protecting their heritage would be characteristic of cities such as Detroit, Akron, Toledo, Cleveland, and Pittsburgh.

---

1 Sherry Lee Linkon and John Russo, *Steel-Town U.S.A.*, (Lawrence: University of Kansas Press, 2002), p. 130

The destruction and dynamiting of Youngstown blast furnaces in the 1980s would start the process of acceptance for the community. Those classic photos seen around the world brought tears to steelworkers everywhere. German steelworkers in the Ruhr Valley were stung that America could destroy the furnaces that had out produced them in World War II. For many, the love of an industry seems strange; but for steelworkers, it truly is a romance. It was a pride for families and the community as a whole. It hurt those who remained. For the older workers, it was far better to leave for Florida, not for a better life, but because it hurt too much to stay. For even a Youngstown reborn without steel would never be their Youngstown.

The Youngstown community enlisted local entrepreneurs, ex-steel managers, and community leaders to bring in new steel plant ownership. Some of the miles of mills were purchased by smaller companies with varying degrees of success. North Star Steel, a mini-mill, purchased the Hunt Steel seamless mill that employed a few hundred employees. Surviving Republic Steel mills closer to Warren were taken over in a merger with LTV Steel in 1984. LTV went bankrupt a few years later and sold the mill. It was renamed Warren Consolidated Industries (WCI). WCI was the last bastion of old integrated steelmaking; in 1939 its blast furnace was the largest in the nation. WCI went bankrupt in 2003. It came out of bankruptcy but was sold to Russian steel maker, Severstal, in 2008, and then sold again. Parts of old U.S. Steel plants became RMI Titanium that lasted into the 1990s. This story of failed revitalization was and is common in the process of de-industrialization because the problem was not management, unions, or even equipment, but an economic policy.

Slowly the Mahoning Valley came to realize that steel was not in the future. The once prized bronze steelmaking monument was moved from the center of a downtown plaza to a new industrial museum in the 1990s. Even there, the monument was split in two. The new steel museum was, in fact, a beautiful tribute to Youngstown's past and demonstrated the city's struggle to move beyond steel. The spiral of de-industrialization in cities like Youngstown was a black hole that seemed to crush all efforts of hope. Ironically, the one improvement in the river valley was the return to its natural settings not seen in more than a century. Unfortunately, this environmental mile marker goes unnoticed in the economic collapse of the surrounding neighborhoods. The broken and boarded up windows on miles of strip mall stores, to some degree, offset the natural improvements. Clean rivers are of little use to the gangs and homeless. The irony is that it reflects the nation's inability for compromise.

The once inflexible Environmental Protection Agency now changed its classifications of hazardous material such as mill slag to help attract new industry to use decades of dumped slag from the mills. Re-training became a career in itself for many steelworkers. Government helped the conversion to new employment by the building of four prisons in the area that employed 16,000 but offered little to community pride. Some felt that prisons, being a growth industry, fit the rocketing rise of crime in the area. The ancillary closings of retail stores left miles of strips of commerce, industrial deserts that spread into the suburbs. De-industrialization changed the demographics of the area, creating segregation and making Youngstown one of the nation's most segregated cities in the United States. Schools collapsed in crime and loss of taxes. Illiteracy reached new heights of 60 percent.

Outsiders often argue that Youngstown needs to let go of it and move on, but they don't understand. The city exemplifies the bond of community and big industry. In many cases, the bond is familial and ancestral. It is cultural, and as seen in Youngstown's churches, it even reached a religious plain. They had memories of labor struggle, but it was struggle with not a wish to destroy the industry. Youngstown, like so many other industrial communities, has industry as part of its past. These cities are like the nations of Europe, which are been leveled and dismembered over the years, only to return to their former borders. The great Ruhr Valley of Germany has seen its steel mills leveled and destroyed over the centuries, only to return. It seems unlikely that the mills of Youngstown will rise again. The unlikely return to steel goes to the very heart of the community which was destroyed. Such moral destruction doesn't come from the bombs that leveled the Ruhr Valley in the 1940s, but from the economic destruction of de-industrialization. Youngstown, however, does struggle with its past and a feeling of betrayal. It will take generations to fully move on; even the environment has shown more versatility in moving on. The reason is generations of proud workers have been reduced to menial work and jobs.

While the Youngstown furnaces and mills have been leveled, there remains one forgotten piece of steel making and American industry that will remain (although forgotten). In the heart of America's rust belt near Youngstown, there is a pantheon of bronze and iron in Niles, Ohio. This pantheon remains today, overlooked at the McKinley Memorial and Library in Niles, Ohio. While lost to the travel guides and tourist trails, it embodies an American spirit of greatness and a time of industrial superiority. It is here that an ironmaster of the 19th century, Joseph Butler, built an architectural monument to a fallen friend and supporter of the industry his beloved President William McKinley. The financial support for such a project came from another admirer of McKinley- nineteenth century steel bad boy, Henry Clay Frick. It is the bust of Henry Clay Frick that fills the prominent place of Steel's Jupiter at the Memorial. Frick, a Pittsburgher, has found no such honor in his hometown or in any American town. Those tears surely were not for McKinley alone, but for golden times. It is Niles, Ohio alone that American industry finds such a place of honor.

In the memorial's 44 bronzes busts is a pantheon of American steel and industry. The busts include great steelmakers and their friends such as Andrew Carnegie, Elbert Gary, Marcus Hanna, Benjamin Jones, Henry Oliver, James Farrell, and John Gates. Other industrialists" busts include Philander Knox, George Westinghouse, and Andrew Mellon. Finally, the presidents that helped build the American steel industry such as William McKinley, Teddy Roosevelt, Howard Taft, and future president Warren Harding are commemorated in the busts and marble columns. This Pantheon is a tribute to the golden years of American industry. Even this great monument has fallen on hard times, lacking funds to have its beautiful museum remain open. The lights will be turned on only by individual request. It is here that the last hope that a youth of a future generation might find inspiration to rebuild industrial America.

Chapter 8. For Whom the Bell Tolls — The Year 1982

The song most often heard on juke boxes in the bars and saloons of America's industrial towns in 1982 was Billy Joel's *Allentown*. It would become the anthem of American de-industrialization. It would talk of how these working families had given their country so much only to be forgotten in their own economic war. It was a country that had asked them to fight global wars only to surrender them in the global war that was devastating their hometowns. The landscapes of their towns now resembled those of Germany after World War II. Part of the motivation for *Allentown* was the closing of Bethlehem Steel's iconic Lackawanna steel plant as well as the closing of the Johnstown, Pennsylvania plant and major cuts near Bethlehem, Pennsylvania. Bethlehem reduced its workforce from 83,000 to 43,900 at the start of 1982. It would turn out to be a brutal year for steel, making the Great Depression look as the good times.

It wasn't just Bethlehem Steel; 1982 was the beginning of the end of the American steel industry. By 1982, de-industrialization had closed 200 steel mills nationwide. Over 200,000 steel jobs had been eliminated, and 140,000 were on laid off. By the end of 1982 for the first time, Bethlehem Steel had more people getting pension checks than pay checks. LTV Steel was only months away from the same tipping point.

The huge seven mile LTV Steel Aliquippa mill outside Pittsburgh went from over 10,000 workers in 1979 to under 500 workers in 1982. United States Steel's famous Mon Valley, the very heart of the Pittsburgh steelmaking, consisted of the open hearth furnaces at Homestead and across the river the Rankin blast furnaces. These Mon Valley furnaces had supplied the battleship steel for our victory in the Spanish–American War, the steel and armor for victories in both world wars, steel for the Brooklyn Bridge, Mackinac Straits Bridge, the World Trade Center, Rockefeller Center, Oakland Bay Bridge, and for the Empire State Building. Mesta Machine's huge complex in Homestead, Pennsylvania, that had supplied the nation's steel mills for so long, filed for bankruptcy.

The year 1982 was devastating to all of the nation's steel industry. Armco Steel closed steel mills in Missouri, Ohio, and Texas. Unemployment peaked in 1982 in Youngstown, Ohio, at 19.7 percent with 46,600 out of work. The statistics for 1982 steel mill towns reflected the same story across America.[1] Some 147,000 steelworkers (hourly and salaried) were on layoff with another 20,000 on short weeks. White collar workers had been forced to accept nearly ten percent in two pay cuts. United States Steel sold its great skyscraper, built in 1980 and the pride of the city of Pittsburgh, to pay debts. Even the United States Steelworkers Union headquarters were forced to cut 200 staffers. Sadly, 1982 was only the beginning of the end.

In that year, the profits in steel were so razor thin that one ladle of steel, out of forty made in a day, had become critical to the month's bottom line. When an Aliquippa LTV steelworker committed suicide by jumping into a 3,000 degree ladle of hot steel, it created a crisis. Everyone realized that the future of the whole plant was in jeopardy in 1982. Traditionally, when a steelworker fell into a ladle of steel, the whole ladle would be buried out of respect. But this time, the 200-ton ladle was suspended in the air by crane as the union and management argued over whether to make product or bury the ladle. Thousands of employees debated as the steel ladle waited. Finally at the last possible minute, the union allowed the ladle to move to the caster to be made into product, while management agreed to bury a small portion.

The year 1982 would end the debate; no one could deny anymore the de-industrialization of America. The 1982 recession was an earthquake caused by a previous decade in which the tectonic plates of global trade had changed the economic map of the world. The 1982 recession wiped out struggling steel, rubber, glass, and manufacturing plants across America, and everything that depended on them. The Big Three auto makers were up to their knees in red ink, and Chrysler was asking Con-

---

1 Christopher G. Hall, *Steel Phoenix: The Fall and Rise of the U. S. Steel Industry*, (New York: St. Martins Press, 1997), p. 74

gress for loans. These were days never even in the Great Depression. The physical infrastructure of America was beginning to decay and the term "rust belt" was coming into use. The devastation was monumental after 1.2 million workers lost their jobs in 2,700 factory shutdowns across the nation. Of the 2,700 closings, 600 were permanent, taking away the jobs of over a quarter of a million people.[1]

This was a tipping point. The auto industry crashed in a matter of months after a brief recovery at the start of the decade. Auto layoffs were over 250,000 by the end of 1982. Total auto employment was down to fewer than 482,000 from its 1978 peak of more than 762,000. The market had shifted to the imports, holding 32 percent versus the start of 1971 at 15 percent. These statistics rippled through a weak economy and the automotive supply chain. The rubber industry was losing major business to imports, in both original and replacement tires. Steel was in a similar position.

Why didn't the politicians do more? One reason was the bipartisan economic bias in favor of free trade imbedded in government and the public discourse. Typical was the view of the Congressional Budget Office in 1982 bills to restrict imports: "It runs counter to the longstanding US objective of promoting open and free trade. . . Using import restrictions to assist beleaguered import competing industries like autos can boomerang and adversely affect US export industries."[2] This was the myth of the Mont Pèlerin international economists.

The auto industry appeared to be lying in ruins. In 1950, American auto makers controlled almost 80 percent of the world market; by 1982, it was under 30 percent. Worse yet, the Japanese had taken 22 percent of the American domestic market; and it would have been higher except for voluntary constraints.

Automotive component suppliers were losing money even faster than the auto companies themselves. All of American industry was declining rapidly. The damage of 1982 would never be restored, and the exports saved would never replace the massive damage done by imports. The formerly high paid industrial workers were now themselves forced to purchase imports as a matter of survival. The struggle of the American middle class workers soon made "buy American" campaigns ineffective.

---

1 "1982 Plant Closings affect 1.2 Million Workers," *News Monitor*, April 1983, Volume 4, Number 4

2 Report by Alice Rivlin, Director of the Congressional Budget Office, before Subcommittee on Trade of the Committee on Ways and Means, September 23, 1982

Trenton, New Jersey, once the iconic home of diversified manufacturing, was falling with the Rubber City and the Steel City. Trenton was typical of hundreds of industrial cities. Once a major East Coast manufacturing center of steel, rubber, machine tools, and pottery, the city had a proud banner "Trenton Makes, The World Takes." Trenton's decline had started after World War II as corporate mergers and a migration out to more livable plant locations drew companies away from the city. Trenton also suffered from the automotive de-industrialization of the late 1970s.

The 1980 closing of the Ford assembly plant at Mahwah, New Jersey, had hurt the whole state. The massive Ford plant in Mahwah had been built in 1955; it was the nation's largest auto plant at the time, covering over 12 football fields. It stood as a symbol of American industrial might. When the plant closed, after many years of struggle, 4,148 workers and 425 managers were let go. Mahwah's closing would make the Country Western charts in a song recorded by Johnny Cash on his "Johnny 99" album. Bruce Springsteen of New Jersey would sing of a Ford worker drowning in gin and taking his life in his 1982 "Nebraska" album.

Social historian John Cumbler noted: "Trenton, New Jersey, offers an opportunity to understand de-industrialization. . . By the 1980s metropolitan Trenton had become an inversion of the medieval fortified city, where peasants and tradespeople ventured out into the countryside during the day only to hurry back to the security of the city by night. Trenton's white-collar workers venture into the city during the day and run back to the security of the suburban countryside at night. Even McDonald's closes after dark."[1] It would describe many cities of the rust belt by the end of 1982 as the loss of manufacturing impacted how we live.

During 1982, for a few days, there was no blast furnace production in Pittsburgh, no rubber made in Akron and no glass made in Toledo. No one alive had known such a day. In fact, for a day that no blast furnace iron was made in the Pittsburgh area one might have to go back 150 years. Unemployment hit 10.8 percent in the nation as car sales plummeted, followed by a crash of the steel and rubber industries. The steel industry put tens of thousands on layoff as industry capacity was running at 48 percent. To the west in Detroit, McLouth Steel went bankrupt. To the north, Republic Steel would close its Buffalo mill permanently.

Weirton Steel in West Virginia announced its closing in 1982. Weirton's massive steel plant produced more tin plate for cans than any

---

1 John T. Cumbler, *A Social History of Economic Decline*, (New Brunswick: Rutgers University Press, 1989), p. 1

other in the world. National Steel's iconic Weirton plant was sold to the employees to prevent permanent closing. Steel industry unemployment was approaching depression levels of 25 percent. The 1982 recession closed thousands of factories that would never open again.

That recession would be the final was the last straw for much of America's heavy industry and more of the industrial core. In the first three months of 1982, over 111,500 steelworkers were laid off. The finality of the closings of many of Youngtown, Ohio's once great steel mills in the 1970s became reality with the front page iconic photos of blast furnaces being demolished via explosion. Alabama's Fairfield steel mill was permanently closed as well as parts of Republic Steel in Ohio. Smaller plants across America closed their gates as auto and steel production plummeted. What had been bad times in the 1970s now became hard times indeed.

In April of 1982, LTV Steel shut down its Pittsburgh Works (formerly Jones and Laughlin Steel) after 135 years of continuous steelmaking.[1] The plant had become, over the last few years, a producer of an intermediate (semi-finished) steel product known as a bloom. The shutdown was considered a "no-brainer" in the vernacular of the time. The blooms produced, even if the workers labored for free, would be more expensive than Brazilian or Russian blooms shipped to Pittsburgh! This amazing result included all transportation costs. This was not free trade but economic warfare. That labor costs were not a significant factor in many industry plant closings was proven in 1982 when 27 factories were closed even after giving wage concessions. Even technology improvements seemed little help against a wave of free trade. It was a war for jobs; and for the most part, America never mounted a serious campaign.

This LTV Pittsburgh steel plant had, just a few years earlier, been converted to new electric furnaces, shutting down the old, expensive blast-furnace/open-hearth furnace steelmaking combination. These were the largest and most productive electric furnaces in the world. Duquesne Light had built a special substation to supply electricity. A continuous caster had been planned just as the 1982 recession hit. This combination would have been the best technology available. The recession and cheap imports would end the great dream of Pittsburgh steelmakers. It would also take the life out of the world's greatest steelmaking valley — the Mon Valley. In the 1940s, this iconic Monongahela River Valley had made more steel than Germany's Ruhr Valley. It was the legendary home

1 Officially idled in 1982 the plant was merely two electric furnaces and a blooming mill – it would operate briefly twice until 1985

of Joe Magarac, the Paul Bunyan of steel. The fall of Pittsburgh Works in 1982 would usher in a decade of steel plant closings in the region.

A few miles up the Monongahela River, the heart of this steel valley, Carrie Furnaces of United States Steel also closed. Now this valley that had out produced the combined steel production of Germany, Japan, and Italy during World War II was on its death bed. It set off a great wave of plant closings, mergers, and bankruptcies moving west to Akron. The plant closing in Pittsburgh ended almost two hundred years of iron and steel production in the "Steel City." LTV Steel reported that the material cost alone, at Pittsburgh, was greater than the total cost of finished Japanese, Russian, and Brazilian steel shipped in to the United States. It was an amazing ending for a plant that once employed 20,000 steelworkers. These were industrial jobs that would never return. What was left of these Pittsburgh managers moved west into the steel mills of Ohio and Chicago, but they found only a short reprieve. By the 1990s, the once great industrial cities of Youngtown, Akron, Warren, Buffalo, Wheeling, Homestead, Braddock, Duquesne, Bessemer, Birmingham, Canton, and Massillon as well as much of the major cities such as Cleveland, Pittsburgh, Detroit, Baltimore, and Chicago were devastated.

The announcement of a possible bankruptcy of the nation's ninth largest steel company, Wheeling-Pittsburgh Steel, struck a new fear in the Pittsburgh area in 1982. Wheeling-Pittsburgh had been modernizing since the late 1960s and had basic oxygen furnaces in place. It had also horizontally integrated into production of pre-fab steel buildings and corrugated sheet products. It was planning a new rail mill in Monessen, Pennsylvania. Having done things right, Wheeling-Pittsburgh was driven to bankruptcy anyway by 1985 as the Japanese brought in rail steel at a lower cost. In 1982, even the union gave wage concessions but to no avail. Free traders called it economically right that cheap Japanese rails flooded the country since the American mills were old and unproductive. Interestingly, after the Japanese secured their dominant role in the steel rail market, there was a dramatic increase in price.

Things were so bad in 1982 that many simply did not believe the problems of the steel companies were real. Some in the union believed the companies had two sets of books and were just playing hardball to get wage concessions. The fall of Youngstown only strengthened the resistance to any cooperation with the steel companies. The big steel companies such as LTV Steel, United States Steel, Republic, Armco, and Bethlehem Steel had deep financial problems with the 1981–1982 recessions, cutting operating capacity to fewer than 50 percent.

Integrated steel mills ran continuously since blast furnaces cannot be slowed down, and shutting down cost $50 million plus. Running at under 65 percent capacity, these huge mills were operating at a loss. Major competition came from both the Japanese steel companies and the new mini-mills. As noted earlier, the Japanese labor costs were half that of the American integrated mills. In addition, the Japanese had more relaxed environmental laws and enjoyed government backing. Japanese laws also allowed cooperation between companies and banks that would not be possible under US anti-trust laws. If this wasn't bad enough, new (mostly foreign owned) mini-mills in the US were taking away the low-quality steel market needed to keep capacity high and operations profitable.

De-industrialization was happening so fast that the mindsets of both the unions and the management could not adapt fast enough. Most believed this was just a downturn, like so many of the industry's 200-year history, and American Steel had survived the Great Depression and many recessions. It was beyond imagination that a United States Steel or General Motors would ever fail. Neither management nor labor knew how to cooperate on the level needed. Neither side realized their fight was not against each other but against a world economic movement advancing under the banner of international capitalism — and they weren't even sure what that meant. For those who loved the industry, the negotiations of the 1980s appeared surreal as both sides seemed willing to go over the cliff wrestling with each other while the free trade politicians were cheering the fighters on. The war had been lost in the halls of academia and bankers conferences. In hindsight wage cuts, more investment, better management, employee participation, and more productivity could not have prevented the demise of the US steel industry.

On July 30, 1982, 400 local union presidents met at the historic William Penn Hotel in Pittsburgh. That was the very hotel built by the infamous union buster, Henry Clay Frick, and the meeting was held there as a statement of how far the union had advanced. Only fifty years before, no union man could have ever hoped to step the inside the gilded ballroom where the rich and famous had danced. In 1982, the Steelworker Union was richer than some of the steel companies. Now they enjoyed the steel city's finest cuisine. Since 1959, the union contracts had been decided in the world's best hotels. Traditionally, both sides pointed to the excesses of the other in trying to win over public support. Democrats and Republicans took their traditional sides. Usually both sides settled on how big the wage and benefit increases were to be every three years. With no major strike since 1959, the Steelworkers' strike fund made it the world's richest union.

The union had been asked by the big steel companies in 1982 to cancel a wage increase in August and accept a three-year wage freeze. The union presidents in a single voice vote shouted down the request in the grand hotel's seventh floor ballroom. It was a statement of anger, when over 107,000 steelworkers were out of work. By the end of 1982, that number would be over 153,000 out of work, equivalent to 53 percent of the workforce; in March of 1983, the union would be forced to accept concessions. The story is not unusual except that both sides were behaving like it was still 1959, with the nation's most powerful companies facing the nation's most powerful union. No one at the time realized what hot water they were in. They were living the popular concept of the 1980s — a paradigm shift.

The steelworkers' convention that fall, in Atlantic City, New Jersey, reflected the destruction of the America's steel industry. United States Steel had just purchased Marathon Oil in an effort to improve cash flow and long term profitability. The union called it a betrayal of the industry, while the owners saw it as necessary for survival. Meanwhile, the union was focused on denouncing the Reagan Administration for the poor economy. Neither side seemed to be looking at solutions for the dying steel mills. Contract negotiations were the pressing matter, but neither side was in a strong position. The workers had exhausted their supplemental unemployment benefits and were against the wall, financially. The millions of dollars in the union's strike fund meant little to the unemployed. The steel companies were so weak that even a short strike could have bankrupted Republic Steel, LTV Steel, and Bethlehem Steel. Industry turned on itself in a quest for survival. General Motors had publicly stated it would increase foreign steel purchases if the steel industry faced a strike. Some felt the Reagan Administration would not allow a strike but would force a settlement. Nobody seemed to know it, but the party was over.

The American steelworker had an estimated $23 an hour in wages and benefits — compared to $13 an hour in Japan and $2 an hour in Korea (below the US minimum wage). Most analysts believed a $5 per hour cut was needed to keep the eight steel company packages at a profitability point.[1] In the end, concessions were made; but the real issues were

---

1 John P. Hoerr, *And The Wolf Finally Came: Decline of the American Steel Industry*, (Pittsburgh: University of Pittsburgh, 1988), p. 344

ignored. De-industrialization continued to sweep through the nation's steel valleys.

The 1983 steel contract was the last one, as industry weakness would require specific company considerations. Both the union and management did compromise, but not on a scale to match the threat they faced. The wage reduction of $2.56 was far too little. The strong dollar maintained by the Federal Reserve wiped out any benefit to the corporations from these wage reductions. The pensions and benefits were not reduced and these now were a huge part of the company's expenses. Most steel companies had more retirees on the rolls than active employees. The settlement, in hindsight, doomed the #2 Bethlehem Steel, #3 LTV Steel, Republic Steel, and other smaller companies and suppliers. Still, it was doubtful that any wage or benefit concessions would have helped for long, short of accepting Third World wages.

Many in steel as well as other industries put their hopes in employee problem-solving teams. LTV Steel found it hard going to convince the union to accept employee teams in 1982. They feared the company unions of the past would get workers involved in negotiating work practices and productivity. The unions limited what the teams could address in cost cutting. In the end, they had little to fear. Japanese-style teams did not fit well in the traditional American management structure. Foremen resisted the teams and resented the access of teams in their area to top management. Plant and middle managers in charge of the teams started to attribute inflated savings to the teams, eroding their credibility. While it was a positive step, the savings needed were beyond the union, management, and the workers to provide. Unfortunately, the problems were beyond the workers or even the management.

Since all countries realized the importance of steel to a nation's economy and employment, any nation that could was expanding steel production to import to the United States. Even our allies, England and the European countries, were dumping steel in U.S. markets. Nearly 60 percent of world steel production was subsidized or government owned in 1982. In Europe, famous steel economist Father William Hogan noted that virtually all "European corporations receive some form of subsidy either for research and development, capital investment, or the so-called emergency subsidies, which often provide funds for operating expenses."[1] In addition, monopolistic vertical arrangements of banks, mining companies, and shippers were legal in other countries, giving them a major

---

1 William T. Hogan, *World Steel in the 1980s*, (Lexington: Lexington Books, 1983), p. 216

edge. Where in America each steel company maintained extremely expensive research centers, other countries had no monopoly laws preventing the sharing of basic research efforts. Efforts in 1981 and 1982 to appeal to international trade organizations such as the International Trade Commission found minimum support for American companies. American politicians, under the advice of the nation's best economists, offered little resistance, fearing trade wars or jeopardizing world peace. It begs the question, in hindsight: 65 years after World War II, would these so-feared trade wars have brought more destruction than the deindustrialization of America, or would the world have been less peaceful without free trade?

In the end, Federal Reverse polices, tariff free trade, overwhelming pension commitments, and foreign nations with strong manufacturing policies destroyed the steel and the rubber industry too. The year 1982 marked the end of tire production in the Rubber City of Akron, Ohio. Imports killed them. General Tire shut down its Plant #1 in March, 1982. B. F. Goodrich Company had gotten out of the tire business in 1975, and Firestone would shock everyone with the closing of plant #1 in 1978 followed by its plant #2 in 1980, ending its passenger tire production in 1980. Firestone would also announce the closing of 14 rubber factories across the nation. Goodyear had stopped tire production in Akron in 1978 as well as Mohawk and Sun Rubber, which also closed that year. These crushing blows virtually destroyed the rubber industry and expedited the fall of the auto industry.

The top of the transportation food chain was hit hard with 400 plants closings and layoffs affecting over 416,000 workers. America's first Japanese car imports arrived at the port of San Francisco in 1959. The imports hit the Western auto industry the hardest that year of 1982, with General Motors closing its Fremont and South Gate plants in California, causing the loss of 20,000 jobs. There were a total of 250,000 autoworkers on indefinite layoff in 1982.

It wasn't just the Northern industries; the Southern textile industry was destroyed. The apparel and textile industry had the highest plant closings with 47 in 1982. One of America's oldest cotton textile mills, Newberry Mills in South Carolina, closed in early 1982. It would be followed by 12 more in South Carolina alone. It was a continuation of the decline of the American textile industry to Mexico, Asia, and China. While the story in the North evolved as a collapse of big-name factories and related cities, the devastation in the South affected primarily small towns and aroused little national concern. Even with the devastation of 1982, few commentators related it to the national effect of globalization and a post-World War II economic emphasis on free trade. Even more symbolic in the South was that the gutting of these small towns occurred without being noticed in most of the United States. Sadly, this great destruction of lives and communities never even got the same national press coverage as the smallest hurricane of the season. This was the screen behind which de-industrialization surged forward — it was viewed as industry specific or regional at the time. The press spread the blame, depending on their political inclination.

CHAPTER 9. RUBBER FALLS

The once great Akron, known as the Rubber City, was the center-piece of one of America's fastest growing metro interstate corridors of Cleveland–Akron–Canton in northeast Ohio by 1970. Akron was a beau-tiful suburban city of metro parks, a national forest, and a cluster of lakes. It functioned as a semi-rural setting for Cleveland executives to the north and a more metro setting for Canton executives from the south. The cor-ridor was pure Americana with the National Soap Box Derby, profes-sional football's Hall of Fame, the World Series of Golf, Bowling's Tour-nament of Champions, and the Goodyear blimp. The corridor had two minor league and one major league baseball teams. Firestone Country Club, at the center of the corridor, hosted the World Series of golf every year, bringing in the best of the world's golfers who haunted the area's best restaurants. Similarly, the week of the NFL's Hall of Fame Game was the nation's party with celebrities filling the hotels and restaurants. The corridor had the more golf courses per capita than anywhere in the nation. It was home to the Professional Bowling Association's jewel — the Tournament of Champions. In the winter, it was home to some of Ohio's only ski slopes. The corridor was not only home to the four major rubber companies but also Timken Roller Bearings, Hoover Sweeper, Republic Steel, Diebold, and many others. Nearby Cleveland ranked with Chicago and Pittsburgh as a major steel center. Most importantly, Akron was the world headquarters of Firestone, Goodrich, Goodyear, Uniroyal, and General Tire for decades.

The Rubber City's core of rubber plants was surrounded by the great steel mills of Cleveland to the north, Youngtown to the east, and Canton to the south. The rubber industry had been the headline of America's industrial prosperity of the twentieth century. It had been an industry that reflected the manufacturing vision of Alexander Hamilton and Henry Clay and the great federal manufacturing policy of the area's native son, President William McKinley. The rubber industry, like the steel and glass industries, had flourished die to a confluence of federal tariffs, individual creativity, American capitalism, and American exceptionalism. Its growth from 1910 to 1920 tripled the Akron area population in a decade. The rubber barons — Harvey Firestone and Frank Seiberling — responded by building neighborhoods, parks, schools, and hospitals. The exclusive Portage Country Club was one of the nation's finest where rubber executives from the top companies ate and played. The same was true of the less exclusive Firestone County Club for all level rubber employees. While there had been struggles with the union, companies like Goodyear and Firestone implicitly promised jobs for life. These companies also rated their executives on civic leadership, requiring executives to be very active in community efforts like United Way.

This story, however, starts with the end of this industrial corridor's prosperity in the 1970s. In 1975, B.F. Goodrich quit making passenger tires in Akron, followed by Goodyear and in 1978, and General Tire in 1982. In 1981, Firestone moved its headquarters from Akron to Chicago. The city and the companies struggled to hold on, but the purchase of Goodrich, Goodyear, and Firestone by foreign companies ended the reign of the Rubber City by 1990. The once great bronze statues of Harvey Firestone and Charles Goodyear were defaced with spray paint and damage. Once middle class neighborhoods started to decline as layoffs rippled through the city. A few miles east, in 1977, the iconic steel plant closed in Youngtown, Ohio, and to the north in Cleveland, Jones & Laughlin Steel faltered, and to the south, rumors of problems with Republic Steel started to surface. America's industrial heart had stopped pumping.

The 1970s dawned with a gathering storm heading to Akron, yet there was no forecast of approaching turbulence. That storm combined high wages, strikes, international competition, an energy crisis, new technology, and aging equipment. The 1970s, however, represented times of high profits for the rubber industry even as these new issues started to show up. In 1976, the industry suffered its longest strike; it lasted 141 days and netted the workers a 36 percent increase in wages and benefits in the next three years. They won the battle and lost the war. These increases would hurt the older plants of Akron first. In 1978, Goodyear closed its Akron tire making while opening new plants in Malaysia and Luxemburg. The companies focused on the new community standard of being a good neighbor by making donations, they didn't invest in the very plants that brought in the money. Goodyear Company would be the most successful of the big four in adapting to globalization.

This very globalization, which was pulling down Akron, had once been the roots of its success. Amazingly in the 1800s, no American industry represented globalization better than the rubber industry that tied the rubber plantations of the Third World to the London rubber markets and to the rubber plants of Ohio. However, by 1975 globalization used Akron as a gateway to the virus of de-industrialization. Looking back for the first sign that the industry was dying, many might point to 1957 when the first Japanese car arrived. The rubber plants of Akron were hit by a perfect storm — cheap global competition, better radial tires that extended product life through new technology, the nation's most generous wage and benefit structure, aging plant equipment, product liability lawsuits, the 1980 recession, and a decline in quality. The industry's management and unions were taken by surprise and proved unable to make significant changes quickly enough. Management was singled out, not for closing rubber plants, but for being too slow to do so. Both the union and management were in a state of denial, refusing to believe that this was a long term trend. But this was a tide that sank all boats.

As noted before, one challenge came from France's Michelin tires, with their new radial technology. The switch from bias tire production to steel belted radial tires in the 1970s proved extremely difficult to emulate. Radials increased product life: Tire life had gone from 2,000 miles with the Model T to 22,000 miles in the 1930s to the 47,000 miles of the radial tire in the late 1970s. Longer tire life cut the tire replacement market in half by 1979. Radials then led to the all-weather tire, which eliminated the snow tire market as well. Radial tires accounted for eight percent of the market already in 1972.

Goodyear had offered a radial tire earlier for the American market, but at that time the auto manufacturers refused to change because of cost: radials would have required car design changes. Then Michelin signed a major deal with Sears, breaking the American market wide open. The auto companies now demanded the American tire companies supply radials. The auto makers were out to save themselves from auto imports and for that, they needed better mileage and radial tires, but in 1973, American tire makers still lacked the equipment and they didn't have the capital to make a quick conversion. By 1976, radials were 45 percent of the tire market. Technology and imports had, in a few years, taken most of the American tire market. Akron was the first pin to be knocked down. The city had the older plants and a history of labor problems.

Pressured to make the change quickly to radials, American tire companies floundered. In 1978, Firestone was forced to recall over 14.5 million new radial tires due to tread separation. The rubber companies found no help from the auto companies or government. The radial conversion forced the shutdown of large bias belted tire plants. B.F. Goodrich Company had gotten out of the tire business in 1975, and Firestone would shock all with the closing plant #1 in 1978 followed by its plant #2 in 1980, ending its passenger tire production in Akron in 1980. The year 1978 was the beginning of the end as small Akron rubber plants such as Mohawk and Sun Rubber closed also. Sun Rubber, a rubber toymaker, had held out longer than most believed it could as Japanese toys was the first wave of globalization.

Goodyear had stopped tire production in Akron in 1978 but had made the switch to radial tires and the global market. Firestone shocked the country with its announcement it was getting out of auto-racing. Firestone tires had been on 49 winners of Indianapolis 500 since 1911and had won the first Indianapolis race in 1909 (a 300 mile race). The results on tire Akron employment were just as devastating. In 1964 there were 37,100 rubber jobs in Akron, in 1970 there were 39,900, in 1974 with the first wave of decline it was 32,700, by 1984 it was 15,400, and finally leveled out in the 1990s around 5,500. Indirectly, hundreds of small supporting businesses went under as well.

The open trade policy of America had flooded imported cars and tires into the American market. This was the same trade approach that had brought down the industry of the British Empire a century earlier. This open trade approach was far different than the McKinley/Republican Tariffs from 1860 to 1930 that had been in place at the zenith of American industry and Akron's rubber industry. It was iconic in that Akron-Canton was the home of President William McKinley, America's greatest proponent of scientific trade protection. The protectionist torch had been passed from Alexander Hamilton to Henry Clay to Abe Lincoln to James Garfield to McKinley; but now the trade policy of Adam Smith had come to be in vogue. The radials led to the all-weather tire which eliminated the snow tire market as well. Technology and imports had, in a few years, taken most of the American tire market. Akron would take most of the hit in terms of jobs as the tire plants shut down.

Small Akron rubber plants such as Mohawk and Sun Rubber (Sun Rubber had made rubber toys) closed also. Goodyear had stopped tire production in Akron in 1978 but had made the switch to radial tires and the global market. Firestone shocked the country with its announcement it was getting out of auto racing. In Akron there were 37,100 rubber jobs in 1964; in 1974 with the first wave of decline, it was 32,700; by 1984, it was 15,400; and it finally leveled out in the 1990s around 5,500. Hundreds of small supporting businesses went under as well.

The destruction of Akron's rubber industry hurt families tied to many businesses in the city. Auto tire production was gone from Akron (although racing tires and tractor tires were still made), and Ohio was left with only Cooper Tire in Findlay (even Cooper Tire had had its roots in Akron). The same men who had devoted so much energy and blood to fighting the nation's wars were abandoned by their government. They no longer had the corporate campaign contributions to interest politicians who had moved on to Silicon Valley and Wall Street banks. But even in defeat, they proved flexible and adaptable. Some moved on, but leaving was too hard for many. They morphed into two-income families, downsized their lifestyles, found work at Wal-Mart. In many cases they became permanent dependents on the social safety net. Others would learn to survive on the streets in the wreckage of a once great city.

In the 1970s when the troubles began, the old tire executives did fight for their city. Rumors at the exclusive Portage Country Club had started in late 1979. At the Firestone Country Club, lower restaurant receipts reflected the depth of the ongoing recession as diners cut back their spending. Others said they had seen downturns before and it was part of life. Technology was making change costly. The belted Firestone 500 tire suffered massive recalls from 1973 to 1979. In 1978, the recall of 8.7 million tires was the largest in history and brought corporate losses of some $700 million, and the company had been borrowing and increasing debt to fund the losses. Insiders were aware of the problem, as were the banks, which had downgraded the company's bond ratings four times. Money for plant upgrades was becoming difficult to obtain.

Firestone president Richard Ripley had struggled to avoid plant closings and layoffs. He was a true Akronite with deep ties to the country clubs, schools, and small businesses. He and his family had lived and played with many of the people whose jobs he was required to cut. Ripley did everything he could to save his beloved Akron from the pain. Ripley watched his own wealth disappear with the drop of Firestone stock in the 1970s. He was cut from the same cloth as the early rubber barons such as Frank Seiberling and Harvey Firestone. The reluctance to close plants was appreciated: "Ripley just lingered and lingered, trying to hold onto the employees; he knew them, their kids, he had golfed with them for years and years."

The Firestone board was less committed to the city and its workers, but they lacked the courage to take the initiative to make the closings. Ripley stood like an Alamo. As was the fashion those days, the board brought in an outsider, John Nevin, to do the necessary dirty work in late 1979. Nevin was a Chicagoan with no ties with Akron. Knowing his role, he took up residence in an apartment outside the five blocks where the rubber executives lived, showing no real interest in joining the community. Nevin lost little time; he closed nine of Firestone's 17 plants in one day, including Firestone's #2 plant in Akron. A few months later, Nevin announced that Firestone would move its headquarters to Chicago. The once great core of the Cleveland–Akron–Canton metro corridor was declining rapidly. Nevin would be called the first of the barbarians of the Cleveland–Akron–Canton corridor. Within a few years, other corporate cost cutters such as Tom Graham at United States Steel and Dave Hoag at LTV Steel would close more local factories.

Like management, the unions tried to save Akron rubber production. In 1979, General Tire's Local 9 forged a new contract meant to address the plague of closings. The union agreed to a decrease of 36 cents an hour, with the money going to a fund to build a more efficient plant in Akron. There would be a seven-day workweek, breaking the long-time tradition of Sundays off. Managers were given more control over who got laid off and how jobs were assigned. It was a forward-looking change for the union, even though it was forged out of desperation. Unfortunately, the flood of cheap imports was unstoppable, and the earlier wage and benefit excesses were too great to overcome. By 1982, the bloodletting continued. Also, Akron was experiencing what most of the nation only today fully understands. High-paying jobs are the underpinning of the economy. When a city loses those jobs, the tax base erodes, and the community felt the pain. Small businesses, schools, community centers, and churches were all hurting. The union and management efforts all failed, making the situation seem hopeless.

In early 1982, General Tire announced it would close the Akron tire plant and return the escrow fund to the workers. General Tire was the last car tire plant in the city. B.F. Goodrich had stopped making car tires in the Rubber City in 1975; Goodyear closed its Akron tire plant in 1978;

and Firestone had closed its Rubber City plant in 1981. General Tire was sold to the Germans.

Imported cars, steel, and rubber had started to increase the loss of domestic industrial business since the early 1970s. Firestone was even forced to sell off Firestone Company Club. The World Series of Golf would have to find new sponsors. The once great area events of the World Series of Golf and the NFL Hall of Fame Weekend were having trouble finding sponsors and money.

Rubber workers and former managers were now in the same unemployment line. The unemployment in Akron exceeded that of the Great Depression. Thousands were forced into early retirement with reduced payments, families forced to move from the part of the country they had loved for generations, and youths stuck in the city gave up on the system — a fact that haunts Akron to this day. High school students were thrown out, and families moved on in search of employment. The related smaller business closings were just as massive and many had no safety net benefits. Some closed factories were made into nightclubs and warehouses. Old strip malls were used as "Halloween haunted houses." Local newspapers blamed poor management, greedy executives, and inflexible unions. The nation, as a whole, took little note, scarcely realizing that this would become a common future for many other regions. Politicians came too late to the real fight. The area's industrial protector, William McKinley, had not found one person to pass the torch to.

The year 1982 was only the exclamation point at the end of a trend that had started in earnest in the 1970s, and that had roots going back even further. The beginning can be traced to a political and economic decision of the United States after World War II to take on a role as the stabilizing force in the world. Part of that decision was a policy to keep the valuation of the dollar high vis-à-vis other currencies. This would make the dollar the reserve currency of the world. This was coupled with an open trade policy to cement trade relationships between nations, on the theory that one is less likely to attack a country that is necessary to one's own economy. However, this combination put basic American products at a price disadvantage. For two decades after the war, devastated European and Japanese steel mills, rubber factories, auto plants, and assembly product lines offered little competition. But as new factories emerged, they offered lower-priced products and flooded the American market. Steel was the first to be knocked to its knees, in the 1960s and 1970s. In the Cleveland–Akron–Canton corridor, rubber was the first to actually fall.

To the south of Akron, in Canton, LTV Steel, in an effort to survive, purchased the venerable Republic Steel. Republic Steel was near collapse in 1984. Now LTV Steel would close its old Pittsburgh-area plants, sending hundreds of displaced managers into the Canton plants to cannibalize them. This was another cloud of worry over the Akron-Canton area. Locals looked at these cold business managers of LTV Steel as a horde of Huns at the south gate of Rome. To the north of Akron, the hordes of LTV Steel executives had taken over the old Republic Steel Building in Cleveland and re-named it after LTV Steel. In Akron, the venerable Firestone Rubber twisted in the wind, selling plants to Bridgestone of Japan in an effort to stay afloat.

Incomes in the Akron area were dropping rapidly. The rubber unions had boasted in the early 1970s that they had the highest wages and best benefits in America. The steel workers' wages had peaked earlier. The Steel Strike of 1959 had been settled by the government to help the union maintain high wages and benefits. Refusal of the rubber unions to recognize the new situation exacerbated the problem in 1982, when the recession was the final blow.

The US auto industry and everything related to it never really had recovered from the OPEC oil embargo. In the Yom Kippur War in October of 1973, the US supported Israel when Arab states tried to take back some of the territories Israel had conquered in 1967. This created a political backlash in the Arab oil producing countries who imposed an embargo on the United States and increased prices to its European allies by 70 percent. Oil jumped from $3 a barrel to over $5 a barrel overnight. By the end of the embargo, it had reached $11 a barrel. Gasoline went from thirty cents a gallon to $1.00 a gallon.

Regional devastation was deep and real estate prices were crushed; but as an aggregate, the American economy absorbed the setbacks in the 1980s and 1990s. Families routinely required two smaller incomes to make up for the loss, but the late 1980s high-technology and personal computer boom helped soften the loss of heavy industry. Steel, rubber, and glass companies tried to adjust with early buyouts to force retirements so plants could be downsized. The highly paid flood of new retirees also cushioned the blow in some communities in the 1980s. But the corporations, carrying the burden of huge pensions, were forced into bankruptcy anyway.

When LTV Steel, the nation's second largest company filed for bankruptcy in 1987, there were five retirees on the books for every active worker. With tens of thousands of retirees, Bethlehem Steel lasted a few more years until filing for bankruptcy. This was typical and only promoted more Chapter 11 bankruptcies so companies could turn their pension liabilities over to the government. By the 1990s, Chapter 11 was hitting the supply chains of steel, glass, and automotive in middle Ohio. Industrial communities such as Akron, Cleveland, Youngstown, Pittsburgh, and Bethlehem were suffering from the loss of taxes, forcing cuts to teachers and school systems.

Most of the nation's rubber plants and steel mills would eventually go down, even with the initial help of Chapter 11 bankruptcy. Those rubber companies that survived were bought out by Japanese companies. In 1988, Bridgestone of Japan would take over Firestone. The automotive industry fared a little better as it got some tariff relief in the 1980s; however, for their own survival, they started to buy from foreign suppliers of steel and other parts. By 1990, it was too late to save the raw material industries of rubber and steel. The auto industry itself wavered, too, but the United States Autoworkers offered some concessions. The auto industry would make it to the next recession in 2007.

Then in 2009, the unthinkable happened with the bankruptcy of General Motors. Detroit had been the fifth largest city in 1950 with 1.85 million people; after General Motors' bankruptcy, it had only 770,000 people left, and they had the lowest literacy rate in the nation, if not in the world. Crime and drugs were so bad the police refused to enter many of the city's neighborhoods. The great "Rust Belt" spread from Pittsburgh and Akron/Cleveland to Detroit and Chicago. Akron stood at the center of it all. In many ways, Akron was America's industrial Rome. Detroit may have been the last to fall, a few decades later, but it was Akron that signaled the beginning of the end.

So who in the end is to be blamed for the fall of industrial Akron? Unfortunately, business analysts have been quick to attack management for their lack of creativity and the unions for their over-the-top demands. But the profits of the companies seemed to justify the wage and benefits at the time. In the 1960s, the auto tire stocks were the darlings of Wall Street with share prices increasing by over 60 percent. The companies were commonly used as case studies for the best in American management. It's hard to blame the unions, either. They had asked little more than a fair share of the growing profits. Nor had these companies ignored technology or plant improvement. But it was only the Southern states with their right-to-work laws and influx of foreign manufacturers bucked the trend of de-industrialization.

Maybe the answer is better seen in the changes that took place within the companies and the industries as a whole, in the relationships between owners, managers and workers, the relationships between company and town. Tom Coyne was an operations manager who had worked under Harvey Firestone, founder of the great paternal rubber company; he set production records; he loved and admired Harvey Firestone. Having worked his way up to management was the proudest achievement of his life. He was a "gum-dipped loyalist." He and his family lived in Firestone Park, a community for company managers. He was proud to live in the "Rubber City." He had worked his way up from the factory floor and had been promoted for his drive and loyalty.

The passing of paternal capitalism dimmed individual motivation and widened the gap between the worker and management. Under Harvey Firestone, the rubber company had hired college-educated managers but never closed the door on promotion through the ranks. A man could rise in the organization based on performance. By the 1960s, with the old lions of Harvey Firestone gone, managers had to have college degrees. The 1960s became an era of de-personalization for American industry. Maybe that change in management is best exemplified by Joyce (Coyne) Dyer's description of her father's demotion at Firestone: "One day in 1962, my dad was told that because he had only a high-school diploma, he was going to be demoted... He was not promotable without a college degree. His salary would necessarily also be reduced, 'you certainly will understand, Tom'." It was a crushing blow. Tom had known and loved Harvey Firestone. He never told his family of the demotion. It would be many years and after his death that the family would know the whole truth.

Within a few years Tom was forced into a union job as the company downsized for its reduced role. Tom Coyne, always proud, ended his career at Firestone as a janitor. Tom remained loyal to the memory of the old company but was devastated by the changes. It was a painful existence that few outside rustbelt families can fully comprehend. Such a thing could not have happened under a Harvey Firestone, but now it was common place. The story of Tom Coyne personalizes de-industrialization. It is often overlooked how many lower and middle managers were destroyed in the wake of de-industrialization while lacking the financial protection of the union.

For many, the management shift of American industry to an international business perspective in the 1960s was when industry lost its heart. This breakdown of the paternal structure would cause major problems in the late 1970s and early 1980s as de-industrialization forced major cost reductions. Once the companies were viewed as family; but when the companies needed the employees to sacrifice in the 1980s and that relationship had to be broken, they recalled their treatment a decade earlier.

The full answer lies with neither management nor labor. Maybe the answer is buried in the mid-Ohio industrial corridor at the McKinley Monument a few miles south of Akron. For years, Congressman McKinley, and later President McKinley, had made his legacy in protecting the rubber, steel, and glass industries. He argued for the principle of reciprocity of trade relations (equal trade dollars between countries), and when necessary, to protect American jobs. McKinley had been the Akron area guardian angel. The Mont Pèlerin Society looked not at reciprocity, but a distribution of wealth to other countries to promote peace. The Mont Pèlerin memorial is in the decaying industrial sections of Akron, Canton, and Cleveland.

Chapter 10. The Mon Valley Collapses

The collapse of the once great Monongahela River Valley of Pittsburgh tells a great deal about the nature and depth of pain from deindustrialization. The Monongahela River Valley, containing the cities of Braddock, Homestead, Donora, Clairton, Ranklin, McKeesport, Duquesne, and Pittsburgh's Southside had 28 blast furnaces operating in the 1950s. At its peak, the Mon Valley mills employed over 120,000. Braddock would become world renowned in steelmaking — on a par with Liverpool, Manchester, Essen of the Ruhr Valley, and Sheffield, England. Within ten years of the opening of Braddock's Edgar Thomson Works in 1875, the mill had broken every world steelmaking record. Andrew Carnegie's Homestead Works would be the world's biggest armor producer for almost a century. Homestead armor would be the key to American naval power from its earliest days in the Spanish–American War. The Jones and Laughlin Southside Works was perhaps the oldest site of continuous steelmaking in America. McKeesport's Duquesne Work's "Big Dorothy" blast furnace was the world's largest in the 1960s.

It was not just steel that fed Pittsburgh, either; the giant Westinghouse plant in East Pittsburgh, which employed 10,000, closed by the end of the 1980s. Other old Mon Valley Westinghouse plants closed, with Air Brake in Wilmerding and Union Switch and Signal in Swissvale.

By World War II, the Monongahela Valley steel operations would out produce the combined production of Germany, Japan, and Italy. Even today, more steel has been made at Braddock than any other place on earth. The industrial riches of Braddock and Homestead drew tens of thousands of immigrant workers to its slums. The Mon Valley was more than a mixing bowl; it was a forge of Pittsburgh's middle class. Immigrant families spent little more than a generation in these slums before moving into middle class jobs. Even the family members that stayed in steel were swept into middle class as the wages increased to the best in the nation. The massive production created the myth of a Paul Bunyan-type Monongahela Valley steelworker known as Joe Magarac.[1] Braddock was the gold boom town of the east; but by the 1970s, it had fallen on hard times. Still, the blast furnaces of Braddock's Edgar Thomson Works had been making iron continuously for steelmaking since 1879. No other place on earth could make such a claim except maybe Krupp Works in Germany's Ruhr Valley.

Steel so dominated this valley that it had its own weather patterns. Local residents during the first six decades of the twentieth century remember the unusual valley snow storms created from massive amounts of steam exuded by the mills on cold winter nights. High pressure often limited sunlight to between 9 am and 3 pm in the summer and 11 am to 2 pm in the winter. Simple thunder clouds would produce complete darkness in midday. Dark days meant bright economic times and were favored by valley residents. In the best of times, 24 hour street lights were required. The orange night glow of the mills from furnace taps was spectacular and rivaled the northern lights of Alaska. The glow of the valley could be seen for a hundred miles east in the Allegheny Mountains. Every youth of the valley knew the daily chore of sweeping mill dust every day from sidewalks and porches. The thickness of the mill dust was used as a measure of economic prosperity. The smell of sulfur was considered part of the environment and another economic indicator. The yellow-brown Mon River also had unique environmental characteristics. The Mon River mill pollution made it un-freezable in the worst of winter. The nature of the Mon Valley made it prone to flash floods in the streams that fed the river that took many lives over the decades. Just as problematic were the legendary spring floods of the river.

The towns of the Mon Valley developed their own social structures as well. The apartments and houses below the railroad tracks and nearest to the river were reserved for new immigrants. The "below the tracks" neighborhoods were first populated by the Irish; and then came the Hungarians and Slavic, then the Italians, and finally the blacks. As immigrants

---

1 Quentin R. Skrabec, *The Boys of Braddock*, (Westminster: Heritage Books, 2004), p. 156

prospered in the mills or became merchants, they moved up "the hill." The religious, family, and cultural ties remained strong. The social and communal activities revolved around church and town. Children of those generations won't talk of the struggle but of happy times. While poor neighborhoods, these were not the ghettoes of today's de-industrialized cities where crime, gunfire, and gangs are commonplace.

The Mon Valley town of Braddock was, at one time, the center of the world's greatest steel industry. The town had been created by the building on Andrew Carnegie's first steel mill. It was on what many considered sacred ground where General Braddock was fatally wounded and his young lieutenant, George Washington, had survived a hail of musket balls. Braddock had grown into a steel town that would rival the city of Pittsburgh for decades, nine miles down the Monongahela. The Braddock mill had made enough railroad rails to travel to and from the moon three times. On Sunday afternoons for the early part of the twentieth century, nearby Kennywood Amusement Park was the terminus of hundreds of streetcars from all over the Pittsburgh District. The streets of Braddock bustled on a twenty-four hour schedule as the mill schedule was 24/7. Braddock was rich with stores and movie theaters. It was a destination for many on a Saturday night. Sadly, Braddock would collapse during the first wave of de-industrialization in the Mon Valley (amazingly, it is today it holds the only surviving mill). That wave ravaged the town of Braddock, leaving three abandoned major movie theaters, two closed department stores, three closed "Five and Tens," and countless retailing and hardware stores. Only bars and churches survived this industrial tsunami of the 1970s. As bad as many Gilded Age journalists pictured Braddock's early steel capitalist days, it would pale by comparison to today's de-industrialized ghetto. Still, the mill remained as the town died.

Some might see little difference between the industrial slums and the later ghettoes, but they are major. Today's ghettoes lack the hope of the old industrial slums. The industrial immigrant slums were a beginning, not an ending. The sons of these immigrant workers often went into skilled trade jobs or management at the mill. Many saved to open bars and stores. Industrial slum dwellers sought and cherished education. They saved money and often sent it back to family in Europe. Crime was not an issue, and people helped each other in the community. Lacking health and disability insurance, they formed their own plans through churches and fraternal organizations. Towns such as Braddock developed a pride of community for decades.

From Thanksgiving in 1979 through the massive closings in the Mon Valley that left only Braddock's Edgar Thomson Works standing, there was more disbelief than action. These venerable mills had been idled many times before, but only temporarily. Even after the iconic mills of the valley fell, one by one, to the monster of the valley, Homestead Works, Homesteaders still expressed disbelief in 1986 that it would close for good. One worker put it this way: "Shock at the news was commonly accompanied by disbelief. Numerous workers reported that they simply had not accepted the company announcement. Among some displaced workers, such denial persisted for years; there were a few persons who, at the time of the interview [1987], continued to insist that the companies would eventually 'come to their senses' and reopen the plants and rehire their former employees."[1] Another historian described the workers beliefs, saying, "They believed that Big Steel would always be there for them, eternal, accepting, inventive, forgiving, and paternal."[2]

That disbelief was in fact common in these company towns, throughout rustbelt plant closings. The idea that the company would change its mind often persisted even after the factories were demolished. There was a presumption that these corporations were too big to fail and the American economy would always bounce back. The mindset of these second-generation European immigrants might have gone back to those European roots as well. The legendary Krupp steel mills of the Ruhr Valley had survived almost four centuries. The Krupp mills survived or were revived after world wars that leveled the works, after political takeovers, depressions, and floods; steel was always made there. Sheffield in England had a similar record as did many towns throughout Europe. Some historic sword-making towns such as Damascus and Toledo had been manufacturing centers since the Dark Ages. De-industrialization on a massive scale was really unknown in the West. Never before had a majority of industrialized countries adopted a long-term economic policy for the re distribution of industry worldwide.

Not surprisingly, this disbelief was shared by union leaders and politicians in these towns. Worker optimism looked for a turnaround or government intervention as a last resort. When companies asked for concessions to keep the factories running, the union turned down the offers, believing the company was bluffing. Politicians also believed in

1 Judith Modell, *A Town Without Steel: Envisioning Homestead*, (Pittsburgh: University of Pittsburgh Press, 1998), p. 255
2 Ellie Wymard, *Talking Steel Towns: The Men and Women of America's Steel Valley*, (Pittsburgh: Carnegie-Mellon Press, 2007), p. 25

the invincibility of the American economy. Local politicians were always seeking a comeback. The road to acceptance was slow and painful.

Communities often looked to retailing or gambling casinos as solutions. The Homestead Mill site would become an upscale mall and entertainment complex in the 1990s, but retailing and gambling have revealed themselves to solve only the immediate problems, for about 20 years. It is heartbreaking to see these once great industrial towns begging for a Wal-Mart, Pro-Bass, or casino to move in. In the end, it is seen that casinos and malls don't create communities, they feed off communities. America seems to have forgotten the role of industry in community building. Still, the Mon Valley believed in a possible comeback.

The Mon Valley had been through hard times before, but never anything like this. De-industrialization not only brought widescale unemployment but stripped families of hope and robbed workers of their pride. The stories of the steel valley in the Depression of the 1930s took on a mythology of their own. Stories of those days of self-reliance and survival were passed to the children of the 1950s and 1960s from their grandparents. In the 1930s, hard times were countered by community, churches, ethnic lodges, small businesses, politicians, and even street gangs. The steelworkers could often get one day of work per week, and they shared with other families their food and housing. To heat their homes, steelworkers took to the nearby hills to dig their own coal and gleaned fallen coal around railroad tracks. One famous street gang, the "forty thieves," turned into a Robin Hood Mission to help families. The gang would steal coal from trains passing up and down the valley and leave loads of coal on doorsteps of the most needy.[1] Local grocery stores extended credit to families. Many families started a local tradition of inviting an unknown struggling worker to Sunday dinner. Landowners extended credit for renters and banks helped those with houses. The steel companies donated to food banks and others supplied heating coal where needed. Ethnic and fraternal lodges helped members cover funeral expenses and insurance payments. Churches and local government held street dances and fairs to supply entertainment for the children of unemployed.

In the end, the 1930s depression proved a triumph of family and community. The mill closings of de-industrialization proved far different. Hope had remained in the 1930s. The Great Depression was a national crisis faced by all Americans with political resolve. The new de-industrialization was a regional and industry-specific phenomenon, or at least it

---

1 Curtis Miner, *Homestead: The Story of a Steel Town*, (Pittsburgh: Historical Society of Western Pennsylvania, 1989), p. 56

was generally framed that way. In the 1930s, workers were "unemployed" steelworkers. They were proud of working in one of the world's most dangerous environments where few could adapt. They took lower jobs for far less money but never lost their pride. During the new de-industrialization, the workers were "ex-steelworkers" without a steel mill. Now, bagging groceries was reality, not a temporary position. This was a personal depression, characterized by demoralizing boredom.[1] This demoralization led to the destruction of the family unit versus the strengthening sometimes seen in the 1930s. Also, during the de-industrialization of the 70s and 80s communities had less of the strong ethnic and religious infrastructure of the 1930s.

Some specific economic reasons for the fall of the Mon Valley were recession, imports, and environmental regulation. The older plants of the Mon Valley were worn down and in need of renovation. The recession made it hard to fund plant upgrades, and competition from imports had cut into what profits were still to be had. And then, any capital available was needed to meet new environmental regulations. The burning of the Cuyahoga River in Cleveland brought national attention to steel mill pollution as a national problem. The Monongahela River was just as polluted; it was less likely to catch fire only because of its strong current. Clearly this was a problem, but massive regulations without a reasonable implementation plan were not quite helpful. In fact, foreign steel was being produced without regard for pollution standards. Steelworkers and managers correctly lamented that a tariff to cover this additional cost was justified. It was an illustration of the error in "free" trade logic that was lost in the analysis of think tank economists.

In that ominous year of 1982, United States Steel purchased Marathon Oil for $6 billion. USS used over $1 billion in precious cash to close the deal. While it would prove to be a long-term investment that helped save the company, it ignited a firestorm given the mill closings and layoffs. After buying Marathon, USS found it extremely difficult to tell the union it lacked funds for modernization. The simple business fact was that the company needed to diversify out of steel to survive. The additional $5 billion in credit would not have been available for an investment in steel. The union and the workers saw this as a betrayal.

Part of the Mon Valley's problem was an inability of management and union leadership to work together or even agree on what they were up against. Historians often trace this labor–management back to the Home-

---

1 Judith Modell, *A Town Without Steel: Envisioning Homestead*, (Pittsburgh: University of Pittsburgh Press, 1998), p. 70

stead Strike of 1892, which had become industry lore. Homestead and the Mon Valley clearly had a radical segment that existed in 1982. This union group was called "the dissidents of 1982."[1] Ron Weisen was the president of the Homestead Local and leader of that radical element. Weisen was an Irish/German second generation steel worker. He was indeed a local historian on the Homestead Strike of 1892. He framed his response in that of the industry of 1892. A union socialist who saw the problem of de-industrialization as a struggle between capitalists and oppressed workers, he loved to take it to the streets. His tactics included burning a cross at the home of United States Steel's president and stuffing dead fish in the deposit boxes of Mellon Bank. He led a group of militants to disrupt Easter services at Pittsburgh's legendary Shadyside Presbyterian Church, once the "cathedral of capitalism." The selection of Shadyside showed his roots in the past. In fact, the once great Shadyside, former home of Carnegie and Henry Clay Frick during the 1892 Strike, had fallen on its own hard times. Weisen gave Democratic politicians a pass, not understanding that government, on both sides, was essentially behind de-industrialization. In fairness, it was a divide that Samuel Gompers had prophesized. The union had made its bed with the Democrats regardless of the politics of de-industrialization, and the Republicans came to oppose the unions as part of the Democrats.

There were other worker dissidents as well. Several rank and file worker movements blamed both the union and management. One of the more positive ones was the Mon Valley Unemployment Committee, which had learned from the collapse of Youngstown in the 1970s. The Committee set up food banks, supplied help with foreclosures, offered psychological help for workers, and addressed the need for political action. These were things the union didn't address, needs the company had dropped with the end of paternal capitalism in the 1930s. Another small group of workers found fault with the government, union, and management. They heard echoes from older Homestead workers going back to the 1870s and the crafts unions and the 1890 McKinley steelworkers. They felt let down by America herself. These workers had probably never heard of the Mont Pèlerin Society, but they knew something bigger than the union or management had changed in America. They understood this was not a 1930s-type depression, but in the popular vernacular of the time, a "paradigm shift." Union leaders had ignored the economic para-

---

1 John P. Hoerr, *And The Wolf Finally Came: Decline of the American Steel Industry*, (Pittsburgh: University of Pittsburgh, 1988), p. 258

digm shift; often their view was limited to the industrial history of the valley.

Homestead had been the flagship of the valley for decades, employ-ing over 20,000 steelworkers and covering almost 400 football fields. In many ways it reflects the very industrialization and de-industrialization of America. Homestead's history was the heart of United States. Home-stead was built by Carnegie's competitors in the 1880s. A new super rail mill, it was to intended to compete with Carnegie's first Edgar Thomson Works, built a few miles up the Mon Valley in 1875. Carnegie's success had brought enemies and jealousy. Pittsburgh Bessemer Steel Company was born out of that competition, survival, and revenge. A group of old aristocratic Pittsburgh steel makers came together to stop the growth of Carnegie after he had taken control of steel companies such as Home-stead's Bessemer Steel from the banks.

The Homestead mill was a Carnegie takeover to take the market from these old aristocrats of the time. Carnegie invested everything in building the best mills or rebuilding older mills. He announced a major rebuild-ing of Homestead Works in 1888 after his takeover, moving it from rail-road production to structural beams to supply the commercial building market. Homestead was to also have the world's largest plate mill for shipbuilding.

Carnegie made plans for the future installation of the new open-hearth steelmaking process which produced higher quality steel than that of Bessemer steel of the earlier Homestead plant. Carnegie had sent his new rising star at Edgar Thomson, Charles Schwab, to Krupp Works of Germany and Schneider Works in France to study the new open-hearth process even though he had already invested millions in the Bes-semer process. Open-hearth, cleaner steelmaking would also bring Carn-egie into the booming market for ship armor plate. Homestead would rule the structural and armor market from 1890 to 1960. Tearing down a two-year-old year plant in order to rebuild it with brand new technology was the hallmark of Carnegie and his organization. They never wasted time when it came to implementing technology.

Carnegie famously tore down a newly built blast furnace to build one with better technology to save a few pennies. Carnegie's famous plant manager of Edgar Thomson works, Bill Jones, referred to it as the "scrap heap" approach. It was an operating philosophy rooted in cost account-ing and a commitment to use anything necessary to reduce unit costs. Carnegie and his 40-plus key manager-partners known as the "Boys of

Braddock" would carry this aggressive policy of technology throughout their careers in various steel companies. These Carnegie boys lived and breathed steelmaking. Most lived and managed in the Mon Valley from 1890 to 1920, embedding the philosophy at Homestead, Braddock, Duquesne, Rankin, and McKeesport. They also had the support and protection of the government to expand this vital industry.

Homestead would be the site of Carnegie's epic battle with labor in 1892. This bloody clash would become the iconic call to arms for the union for decades to come. The Homestead Strike of 1892 would scar the great philanthropic works of Carnegie and his partners. Still, Carnegie and his partners were steel men; they had invested all of their profits back into steel mills. The re-vestment of profits back into steel operations became a bone of contention among other partners. Eventually, the internal split would lead to the takeover by J.P. Morgan's New York bank. Homestead had been a major step in the industrialization of America and the formation of United States Steel in 1901. The banks once again would control steel, but it took decades for the banks to tame the old operating lions.

Carnegie, Ford, and Firestone were examples of capitalists that believe in rapid implementation of the latest technology, often against the advice of their bankers. They feared the day bankers might control the boards. Carnegie would eventually sell out to banker J.P. Morgan to form United States Steel, assuring that his managers would control the operations of the new company. Many of Carnegie's greatest managers such as Charles Schwab would find difficulty in working for a bank-controlled company. The Carnegie Steel Division of United States Steel, which controlled the Mon Valley, remained true to the Carnegie vision into the 1950s. Still, banking interests had changed steel as Carnegie had predicted they would. Henry Ford had also feared banks making financial decisions over operations men. The great paternal capitalists were operations men, making decisions that would reduce product costs and improve quality.

Interestingly, the 1982 radicals of the era of de-industrialization had identified similar elements that had been operating below the radar. Most Americans have always looked at banks and big business as the same entity; but that is far from the truth. Bankers lacked the passion that was common in any great industry. Banks were behind not only the diversification movement of domestic steelmakers, but the development of external competition. American international banks were supplying capital to Japanese steelmakers while lobbying Washington for free trade. Between 1975 and 1977: "Citibank increased its loans to Japanese steel from $59 million to over $230 million. Chase Manhattan's investments in Japanese steel rose from $59 million to over $204 million. And the loans from the Chemical Bank of New York increased more than five times."[1] The banks were the biggest supporters of the Mont Pèlerin Society's premise that capitalism was international and could not be practiced on a single nation level.

The workers in Homestead knew something smelled fishy about the banks. They would have agreed with Henry Ford who said, "Bankers play far too great a part in the conduct of industry. Most business men will privately admit that fact. They will seldom publicly admit it because they are afraid of bankers."[2] The banks watched as the union and management blamed each other and both blamed the government. More importantly, the bankers helped strengthen the opposition of the two.

That opposition would play a key role in the failure of the steel industries. The 1982 dissidents strengthened resistance to any compromise that some historians believe could have saved the Mon Valley. One of those was John Hoerr, who summarized in 1982: "The inability of the steel industry and the union to help each other stave off disaster in 1982 arose partly because the forms of democracy, both in the mills and in the union, had not been converted to a political reality which could comprehend economic reality. Long ago union and management leaders had shunned an approach that might have produced a vastly different result in 1982."[3] Hoerr's remark was made in 1988. We can now see that deindustrialization was bigger than any possible union agreement, and one in 1982 would have been temporary.

The situation was better understood in 1982 at Homestead's Mon Valley neighbor — J&L's Southside works. Southside Works had newly installed electric furnaces, which were the world's largest and most productive. They had been built with the hope of installing a continuous slab caster, but the capital shortage of the recession forestalled that. The hard fact was that J&L could buy steel slabs shipped to Pittsburgh cheaper than it could produce them at Southside even if the workers worked for free.[4] Economists could argue free trade philosophy and the politicians spoke about the big picture, but the fact was steel was being

1 Barry Bluestone and Bennett Harrison, *The Deindustrialization of America*, (New York: Basic Books, 1982), p.144
2 Henry Ford, *My Life and Times*, (New York: Doubleday, 1924), p. 176
3 John P. Hoerr, *And The Wolf Finally Came: Decline of the American Steel Industry*, (Pittsburgh: University of Pittsburgh, 1988), p. 260
4 This is from the personal files of the author who was manager of Quality at J&L Southside and Pittsburgh Works at the time

shipped to the United States at slightly less than the raw materials costs. To the steelworker, that fact proved foreign steel was being subsidized by someone. This was a problem that management and union concessions could not solve. Unfortunately, economists and politicians found it convenient to believe they could.

The reduction of the once giant steelmaker, United States Steel, meant more than lost mills and union workers. It hit white collar and management with the same fury. Between 1982 and 1986, United States Steel cut its salaried non-union employees from 20,837 to 7,736. In the Mon Valley alone, the president of United States Steel, Thomas Graham, decreed a 50 percent reduction of supervisors and staff in 1983. The permanent cuts were followed by demotions for those who remained. Lower level managers were demoted to back shift foremen. The cruelty of these supervisor cuts far exceeded that of the union steelworkers that the press wrote about. Notices were less than 24 hours; often the supervisor worked his last shift only to be called in and fired. LTV Steel followed USS's lead. At LTV, supervisors were called in, terminated, then escorted by company guards to get their personal items and shown out the gate. The company feared they would respond with rage, and damage property, but instead shock and tears were the most common response. Many of these supervisors had worked for the company for decades.

The fall of the Mon Valley brought a new type of urgency to United States Steel's management as well as the other companies. Not only was the $23 an hour labor cost a problem, but Japanese used about 3 man-hours per ton of steel to 7.5 man-hours in American steel mills. The 1983 steel industry-wide contact did little to actually reduce the $23 an hour issue, forcing management to look for productivity gains to offset the wage/benefit disadvantage. Part of their research resulted in a major management revelation, but it would do little to save decent jobs. Frantic trips to Japanese mills by Mon Valley managers revealed the part of the productivity advantage came from outsourcing the menial jobs as well as maintenance. American steel outsourced more jobs to meet the Japanese. The result was even more ex-steelworkers.

The ex-steelworkers of de-industrialization were alone in many ways. The nation saw it as a steel industry problem, and the country was moving on to an information age. Steelworkers were viewed as social dinosaurs following their fathers and grandparents to the mill instead of improving themselves. They were uneducated, and the government viewed them that way. Millions of dollars were supplied for endless retraining that rarely resulted in an ex-steelworker landing a new job.

Communities were criticized for their failure to diversify into multiple industries. Ex-steelworkers were told they were inflexible because they wanted to stay in the area they loved.

A few like Republican Senator John Heinz crossed ideological lines, realizing we needed a national manufacturing policy and leadership; but for the most part, it was too little, too late. It all supplied some anger for the ex-steelworkers; but after a few years, identifying reasons and causes did little to ease the crushing personal demoralization. Unions dug in to resist management pressure, since all their earlier cooperation had not gotten them anywhere.

The steelworker and rubber worker unions had also fallen to the prediction of Samuel Gompers, the father of American unions. Gompers had strongly advised unions to stay out of politics; he particularly advised against alignment with any one party. Gompers had seen the socialists of Europe take over the union, making it a political tool. American unions, until the 1930s, had avoided strong irreversible ties with any particular party. Instead, politicians were forced to cater to the union vote, which could change with each election cycle. Since the 1880s, union leadership did tend to favor Democrats; but members didn't always follow, and large financial support via member dues had at least publically been avoided. The rise of powerful national unions changed all that. The AFL-CIO unions of the rust belt became political agents and aligned with the Democrat Party.

At the start of the 1930s, less than 10 percent of America's labor force was unionized; after the 1935 passage of the Wagner Act, the decade ended with 35 percent of the labor force unionized. The progressives in the Democratic Party had led the effort to pass the Wagner Act. The Act changed the role of government in labor policy. The act declared that democracy must apply in the workplace. Furthermore, the Act declared the means to this democracy was the right of workers to organize and bargain collectively through employee representatives. The Act established a National Labor Relations Board (NLRB) to implement and oversee the Wagner Act.

Unionization in America had had a very difficult path up until then. In steel, unionization had been beaten back in the 1893 Homestead Strike and the Great Steel Strike of 1919. Unionization had been declining in all industries after 1919. Automotive had a less bloody history, but unionization had also been stalled. The electrical industry also had many failed attempts at unionization. Progressive liberal Democrats had continued the fight, but even Woodrow Wilson's War Labor Boards during World

War I, with war powers, could not overcome the industrial owners. The Great Depression brought on more social unrest and union activity. New York, in particular, was a hot bed of unions, socialists, and communists, who said the workers were not getting their share. Progressives and conservatives alike feared the influence of European socialists and communists, but agreed that labor was being treated unfairly. Many complained of the using of spies, the firing of suspected union organizers, and blacklisting by the companies. Even enlightened managers such as John D. Rockefeller and Charles Schwab realized that employees somehow needed to be brought into wage and work disputes. The union movement was fractured between John Lewis's Committee for Industrial Organization (CIO) and the American Federation of Labor fighting for the representation rights in the steel and automotive industries. The New Deal Democrats and Progressive Republicans thought it was necessary to take a bold step into labor policy to hold off Roosevelt's progressives. Without addressing labor issues, the economic downturn and the rise of communism in Europe, which promised better housing and services for workers, raised many fears that more serious social unrest might come to the United States.

Interestingly, the Wagner Act did not apply to government workers and supervisors. Federal workers remain today one area where strikes have been restricted. The National Labor Relations Act was, to some degree, an overreaction; balance would be achieved after years of debate and amending. It was hoped that the Act would improve the economy by increasing wages; this was never achieved.

The first major union success came in 1937 with the victory of the CIO union over General Motors, followed by the unionization of United States Steel Company. The heart of the Act is section 7: "Employees shall have the right to form, join, or assist labor organizations, to bargain collectively through representatives of their own choosing, and to engage in other concerted activities for the purpose of collective bargaining or other mutual aid and protection." The key was a secret ballot election of the union under the auspices of the National Labor Relations Board (NLRB). Since the passage of the Wagner Act, there have been over 360,000 secret ballot elections. The NLRB has five members appointed by the president with Senate oversight. Early on, employers and the AFL, which argued CIO unions were favored, questioned the neutrality of the NLRB. Neutrality had proved difficult over the years. Even President Roosevelt was concerned that the Act went too far. Still, companies had also gone too far in restricting employee representation. The National Labor Relations

Act would face 20 years of challenges in Congress, but the conflict forged a political and operating alliance between the Democrats and the union. Two major amendments would be the Taft-Hartley Act in 1947 and the Landrum-Griffin Act in 1959. The National Labor Relations Board today remains a type of court for employee complaints. The struggle of board members continues to this day.

During the 1940s, 1950s, and 1960s, and into the 1970s, the industrial unions sat at the main table of the Democratic Party. It had become a symbiotic relationship, with the unions supplying votes and money. It would prove to be a major political problem in the long run, dividing Congress and the nation. It also in a strange way would mute the unions' power to fight against free trade as Democrats joined the free trade movement in spite of them. Politicians tending to favor the powerful and steelworkers were past their prime, having little votes or money.

As de-industrialization sweep though the industrial heart land, the steel union needed to build political alliances in Congress, but its association with the Democratic Party now prevented this. The relationship of the union with one party managed to split what would have been a domestic and patriotic support in Congress. It affected even the union's Buy-American campaigns as Southern highly patriotic Republicans, who would normally buy American, resented the money going to defeat Republicans. This was exactly what Samuel Gompers had foreseen and feared. Furthermore, as heavy industry declined, the big unions had less votes and less money. Eventually, some industrial unions had to give up their seats at the party table to the fast growing government unions. The industrial unions were now dependent totally on the Democrat party, and the Republicans were united against both. Only the most popular Republicans, such as John Heinz in Pittsburgh, dared to cross the Republican leadership. Similarly, it was extremely rare that the union leadership would support even the most friendly and supportive Republican politician. Unions had defined themselves as the Democratic Party money machine. Unfortunately, the political split in the end prevented a political solution.

Politicians had proved little help in the long run. Unions had become an integral part of the Democratic Party and made the party dominant for decades. The Democratic Party owed its very existence to unions; and in the 1930s, the Steelworkers were the largest union. As industrial union membership declined, the Democratic Party became the leader of the unions. Slowly the Democratic Party gave way on free trade as steel declined. As union money poured in to defeat Republicans across the nation, Republicans became less interested in compromise and more interested in promoting non-union transplant companies in the south. It was a nation turned on itself via politics.

Politicians who had once stood at the steel mill gates on election days, asking for votes, realized the votes were gone. At the last days in the Mon Valley, those who gathered at the mill gates were not politicians but tearful families. Like their great and great-great grandfathers who entered these mills alone, they left alone in the 1990s. Industrial unions continued to lose power within the Democratic Party, allowing President Clinton to move to free trade. By then the unions had nowhere to go but the Democratic Party. By 2000, the free trade argument had been lost for good except on a symbolic basis. George Bush would extend some protection and tariffs for the steel industry, but the United Steelworkers could not find it in their hearts to credit him for the help.

Today there is no longer any steel industry to protect, and overall industrial unions continue to decline.

CHAPTER 11. THE HEARTLAND FEELS THE PAIN

There is no good explanation for America's lack of concern for its industrial assets. The 1980s saw a destruction of industry and manufacturing throughout the country. The combination of imports, recession, and the super dollar laid waste to the manufacturing heartland. The super dollar, in particular, allowed cheaper imports to take over the market even in big-ticket items such as construction equipment, machine tools, and farm equipment. The strong dollar made our products even more over-priced as export items. By the mid to late 1980s, Japan and Europe were selling these equipment products at prices 20 to 40 percent less than American production costs![1] This was an amazing but a common problem in the 1980s. The high valuation of the dollar made wage levels irrelevant. In addition, most industrial nations had an overall policy or strategy for manufacturing, and America seemed to lack any coordinated approach. The 1980s and 1990s, to an outsider looking at the economic indices would have to conclude that there was a policy of de-industrialization in place.

Between 1980 and 1985, the dollar rose 60 percent, making American exports costly and uncompetitive and imports cheap. For Americans who were not part of the industrial manufacturing system, this meant that all kinds of household goods were suddenly very affordable. But the wave of de-industrialization now moved from the big cities and indus-

---

1 Patrick F. Doumit, "The U.S. Machine Tool Industry," The Industrial College of Armed Forces, Washington D. C., 1993.

tries to Midwestern towns. This wave accelerated as China became an industrial player in the 1990s. Small towns such as Celina, Ohio, which had for years been the home of the world's largest bicycle manufacturer, Huffy Bicycle, saw the bicycle factory give way to Chinese imports. In the South, furniture manufacturers were moving off-shore, leaving small towns without work. Forging plants were also leaving small Midwestern towns. The same was happening all over America by the 1990s, but without the fireworks that marked the changes in Youngstown or the Mon Valley.

The pain of the heartland had spread to its anchor city of Chicago in 1980. The South Side of Chicago was hit hard as the early recession of the 1980s closed parts of the integrated mills of United States Steel. The beginning of the end for Chicago's came in the captive steel casting and forging steel manufacturer of International Harvester, Wisconsin Steel. Wisconsin Steel represented the Chicago's great mix of industry and agriculture. At its peak, it employed 5,000 employees in Southeast Chicago. The plant had been operating since the late 1800s, making steel components for International Harvester. The plant was operating at a loss in the 1970s. A popular strategy at the time was to divest suppliers in hopes of reducing costs. The plant was sold in 1977 to Envirodyne which was supposed to serve as an outside supplier to International Harvester. The move forced Wisconsin Steel to compete in the low-labor-cost global market. They struggled for another three years before closing in 1980. It would be the beginning of the demise of South Chicago and Indiana as the center of steelmaking.

The second blow to Chicago's Southside came in the 1980s with the closing of United States Steel's South Works. Again the union was shocked by the swiftness of de-industrialization. The Chicago rail mill had been part of the targeting of the Japanese to undercut and take over the railroad rail market. The union in Chicago not only rejected concessions (although the talks were poorly managed by USS executives), but went to court to block the use of imported semi-finished steel. Semi-finished imported steel could be purchased at a great cost saving over that made in America. This semi-finished steel could then be used in American rolling mills to produce a competitive product. Of course, this was no help to the union since it would sell out the steelmaking work, where most of the union workers were employed. In hindsight, while the use of semi-finished still would have destroyed the industry in the long run, it might have allowed a more gradual transition.

The fall of the Mon Valley in the Pittsburgh area had slowed the decline of the Chicago steel district as production shifted west. De-industrialization of manufacturing, however, had moved west also. The problems of South Chicago seemed distant to small town America in the 1980s; no one realized this was a systematic cancer that would attack all types of manufacturing. The term *globalization* was becoming popular; perhaps there was an underlying confidence that America would continue in its leadership role. Globalization became, to a large degree, accepted as an inevitable course of the world. The economics behind it were beyond the understanding of main street America.

Another part of the acceptance of globalization was rooted in the decline of American nationalism after Vietnam. The countries that succeeded under globalization were, in fact, very nationalistic in terms of policy. Japan and later China showed how to take advantage of globalization. Even the Mont Pèlerin group in the 1940s never foresaw this type of economic warfare. Mont Pèlerin saw reciprocal trade as a means to eliminate wars. It would have been hard for them to imagine that the economic attacks of the 1980s could produce more devastation than the bombs of World War II.

The poster girl for de-industrialized heartland America is Fostoria, Ohio, once a glass town and the crossing point of five major railroads known as the "iron triangle." The editor of *Harper's Magazine* called Fostoria, "a small town in the middle of everywhere." Fostoria's rail crossings and natural gas deposits made it a magnet for factories. By 1920, it had 13 glass factories, but these moved out before World War II. Until 1920, Fostoria was a major producer of light bulbs for General Electric. The loss of natural gas pressure caused a mass exodus of the glass plants. One of the most famous — Fostoria Glass — kept the name while moving to West Virginia.

Fostoria survived and retooled after this first de-industrialization. In the 1930s, Autolite Spark Plug built a factory there and prospered. Fostoria became the "Spark Plug Capital of the World." Other industries such as Atlas Crankshaft and Fostoria Industries (an oven producer) came, and the town grew from 10,000 in 1920 to 16,000 in 1970. Fostoria has the feel and look of a larger industrial city. Its industries struggled through the slow and painful decline from 1977 on. First, as with big industry, international companies bought up local manufactures and tried to streamline them into profitability. Then there were further forced reductions as ThyssenKrupp purchased Atlas and Allied Signal purchased

Autolite. Finally, the North American Free Trade Agreement brought cheap labor in to compete directly with Fostoria's workers.

One of the great triumphs of the Mont Pèlerin Society, NAFTA, brought the end of industrial Fostoria and changed small towns all over America. NAFTA in 1993 represented a final political victory of Mont Pèlerin Society as the Democratic Party fully embraced free trade. The Republicans had embraced free trade under Reagan. President Bush and President Clinton both agreed on NAFTA. No political party challenged free trade, except the followers of the neo-Whig, anti-NAFTA politician Ross Perot. Autolite's competitors moved to Mexico, making spark plugs much cheaper. In addition, the overall demand for spark plugs dropped as the long life platinum plugs took over the auto spark. Spark plugs faced the same double punch that had hit the tire industry (expanded product life and imports). Spark life went from 12,000 miles to over 100,000, basically eliminating the replacement market. Still, the market was highly profitable if you had Mexican labor costs.

Unionized Fostoria workers averaged $22 an hour with benefits while workers in Mexicali were getting about $2. In addition the standard work week in Mexicali was 48 hours versus 40. By 2009, the employees numbered under 120 in Fostoria. The company offered a deal to take wages to $11 an hour with a major increase in the health care deductible. The union balked, preferring to negotiate better severance benefits. The plant hung in with about 80 employees left, making ceramic boot insulators for the plugs. Like the rubber and steel cities, small manufacturing towns became industrial deserts.

Fostoria still has many freight trains blocking traffic as goods move through to other destinations. The city blocks are striking similar to Detroit or Toledo but lack the services of vital infrastructure. There are empty lots, boarded up houses, trash, and crime. Businesses have closed in the downtown area. Homeless people roam the streets. Rusted rails are increasing as the railroads are pulling out of the Rust Belt. The "iron triangle," the symbol of Fostoria's industry, is covered with trash. Fostoria is today's typical small town lacking manufacturing.

In the Carolinas, the story is similar as the Southern textile industry has been in slow decline since the 1950s. Ironically, the Southern textile industry was a product of nineteenth century internal globalization. Initially, like steel and rubber, global wage competition created mergers and takeovers of weaker domestic competition. Technology was improved, but this only masked the longer term problem of very cheap labor elsewhere in the world. Textiles had fought a tough battle for decades with the Southeast Asia, India, and the Caribbean Basin. The 1990s brought new tigers into the fight — China and Mexico. Like steel, textiles were given a patchwork of various tariffs that only slowed the decline. The Southern textile industry would fight waves of globalization. They held off the first Asian competitors with reduced wages and benefits and improved technology that boosted productivity, they moved to non-union labor, and won some support through tariffs. During the 1990s, however, free trade agreements such as NAFTA hit the textile industry hard, the declining valuation of Asian currencies made their products cheap for Americans, and major purchasing agreements from the likes of Wal-Mart undercut traditional cost and price arrangements.

NAFTA and Wal-Mart were the primary drivers for the major decline of the 1990s.

NAFTA is a story unto its own. NAFTA is an example of how de-industrialization was able to maneuver between the parties, allowing the political divide to move de-industrialization forward. NATFA was what union founder Samuel Gompers had foreseen as the destruction of the union movement. The unions had aligned themselves strongly with the Democrats since the 1940s. Union money was being used against Republicans who now were aligned with the "right-to-work" Southern states. When President Clinton followed the advice of his economic advisors to implement NAFTA, the union had little recourse. It argued, but it could neither go to the Republicans or threaten withholding money to the Democrats. This was a bitter pill for the union. Part of the sales pitch was that Mexican cheap labor was a much bigger threat to non-union Southern labor. Nobody, not even Clinton, realized the number of Fostorias that would be created in the North. It was the South and non-union in textiles that took the first blow, but auto suppliers soon starting moving to Mexico as well.

Free trade zones such as the European Union and NAFTA had been the dream of the Mont Pèlerin Society. Tariffs had successfully slowed the Asian invasion into the textiles, but NAFTA would give cheap Mexican labor the ability to compete. NAFTA accelerated the major decline of US textiles; the horseman of globalization had a number of other weapons as well. A decline in the value of Asian currency and the entrance of China would prove even more devastating than NAFTA. During the period from 1997 to 2002, over 100,000 textile jobs were lost in the small towns of North Carolina, on top of the 82,000 lost from 1977 to 1997. And the nation has lost an amazing 700,000 jobs in textiles just since 2000. The loss of textile jobs in small towns exceeded that in rubber and steel.

Wal-Mart was part of the acceleration of job loss in textiles. Wal-Mart made huge bulk purchases that favored the cheap labor costs and plant networks in China. Another problem was the time-bomb approach taken by the World Trade Organization, which offered declining tariffs to allow the American industry a little time to "modernize." This approach was typical of the WTO, which would stall and then allow tariffs to phase out. The approach only diffused political opposition; it did not help industry. The manufacturers did, in fact, invest in new technology, but discrepancy in labor costs outweighed any possible increase in efficiency. Furthermore, the loss of non-union textile jobs was of little interest to union politicians. The battle now was over Wal-Mart's non-union internal practices, not tariff-free trade and international labor inequalities. America divided cannot compete with the unity of interest that gives strength to the tiger of China.

The North Carolina town of Mount Airy exemplifies the decline of small textile towns in America. Mount Airy is best known as the birthplace of Andy Griffith and was the model for the TV fictional town of Mayberry. Mount Airy's city seal features the four foundations of the local economy — textiles, tobacco, furniture, and granite blocks. De-industrialization has destroyed all those pillars.

Mount Airy is located in Surry County, which has lost 10,000 jobs in the last ten years. Textile workers in the Mount Airy area earned $15 an hour but are now are happy to find any work at all. The unemployment rate in 2013 is above 12 percent; small-town people have deep roots and cannot simply drive away. The story of textile de-industrialization can be read page by page, town by town. And still, Americans seemed numb to the loss of her small manufacturing.

The indoctrination of university trained Mont Pèlerin economists still runs deep. People amazingly see globalization as modern and inevitable, something that must be stoically accepted. A plant manager near Mount Airy and a graduate in economics justified the loss of textile jobs: "I understand that free trade opens the door for [other] American businesses."[1] It is amazing that after 50 years of job losses and de-industrialization, Americans, even in these devastated areas, talk of free trade being good for business. In the South, this acceptance seems related to their allegiance to the Republican Party. Mainstream Republicans consistently promote the view that "free" trade is necessary for capitalism, completely burying their almost 100-year commitment to protecting

1 Paul Wiseman, "When the Textile Mills Goes, so does the Way of Life," *USA TODAY.com*, March 9, 2010

American industry. This may be good for international businesses and the bankers' capital that funds them, but it is far from good for Americans who have to work for a living.

North Carolina was then hit with the decline of the furniture industry, when the job opportunities all migrated to China and Mexico. High Point, North Carolina, was "the Furniture Capital of the World" in 1990. With its huge semi-annual exhibition, High Point, a mid-size city, is emblematic of the North Carolina furniture industry. The decline of the furniture industry is a relatively recent wave in de-industrialization, but the same old story is clearly playing out again. The industry is bombarded with ideas on how to save itself and compete with China. One industry journal talks of the need to innovate and adopt new manufacturing methods — while noting that the average American furniture worker makes $14.00 an hour versus the 69 cents of the Chinese worker.[1] This doesn't even account for the commercial support of the Chinese government. Southern non-union labor is the most competitive in the US, and yet obviously they could not survive on income anything close to that of Chinese labor. The job losses in the counties surrounding High Point reflect this international inequality.

North Carolina does offer some insight in how small town America absorbs these huge job losses with an uprising.

Yet the American culture always promotes a hopeful outlook; and a belief, based on our history, that the future always brings something brighter. It many ways it has become a sad story. The local community college is thriving as older workers strain to meet the requirements for new careers. If they can complete their courses, many of these graduates will have to travel up to 80 miles to find work. Many of them are training for government jobs, the only thing that so far has resisted outsourcing — but state and municipal budget cuts signal a shrinking field there, too. Many workers in America have been re-trained numerous times for new and "better" jobs, albeit at lower and lower wages. One local government strategy is to become a wine-producing area. Vineyards are being planted, and the community college is offering courses. Of course, it takes years for a vineyard to start real production; but such hopeful future industries are illusory anyway. Wine-making is labor intensive, leaving it open to global competition. Even the green jobs that were once hailed as not being able to export are, in fact, being exported. China has overtaken American in the production of solar panels and wind mills.

---

1 "North Carolina in the Global Economy," *Furniture*, August 27, 2007

Our non-union workers still vote Republican while their union counterparts in de-industrialized North vote Democratic, which is testimony to the power of political polarization over de-industrialization. America is blinkered by misunderstood or false political divides that seem more important to voters than the reality of the economy. This divide runs against logic, like the feud between the Hatfields and McCoys. America clearly needs a national strategy that supersedes party affiliations, yet neither party seems to have any interest, and only the parties can capture voters' attention. Since the Whig Party of the 1800s, the American worker has no party committed to jobs above all.

The decline of the glass industry has affected small town America just like textiles. In 1960, small glass companies were spread throughout Indiana, Ohio, West Virginia, New Jersey, and Pennsylvania. Glass is a much segmented industry made up of novelty glass, tumblers, jars, bottles, auto plate glass, and flat window glass. Glass had been made at Jamestown in the 1600s, making it America's first industry. Then, in the early days of the republic, the industry was all but wiped out by imported glass. Henry Clay championed its return in the 1830s. An abundance of silica, and forests for fuel, had made glassmaking in South Jersey an obvious choice. Towns like Glassboro, New Jersey, and Corning, New York, focused on glassmaking. Then the de-industrialization of the 1970s took down the small novelty glass and tumbler markets. The loss of these small novelty glass companies passed on their pain to the specialty steel and foundry industry, since high alloy cast steel glass molds were big business. The 1980s saw further declines with cans taking away from the glass jar business. The decline accelerated in the 1990s for glass as for textiles, as Mexican cheap labor was coming into play. The final blow was the loss of the flat glass market. From 2001 to 2008, the American glass industry lost over 40,000 workers.

The building that houses a glass museum in Toledo, Ohio, once America's "Glass City," was built in the 1990s and used special glass from Japan. How symbolic. A decade later in the building that replaced New York's Twin Towers, Chinese glass was used in the lower 20 stories. The original Twin Towers had been 100 percent American-made glass. Foreign-made flat glass, once considered to have natural protection because overseas transportation would risk breakage, was now cheaper. In fact, some glass can be shipped to America cheaper than glass made with American workers working for free. Even in Florida, the glass for the most competitive hurricane windows comes from South America. Here, China has no major advantage in raw materials or energy. Economists may make sense out of this, but common sense tells us it is not possible without government support or currency manipulation. Glass production has also been reduced due to the importing of cars and furniture. There is little left.

The pain to small town America is equal to that of our cities. These towns hold the shells of empty small businesses. Some people have returned to the family farm, if it still exists. Schools are losing ground as the tax base is eroded. Wal-Marts offer jobs for a few, but the arrival of a Wal-Mart generally spells the death of downtown, and retailing never leads an economic turnaround.

CHAPTER 12. BARBARIANS AT THE GATE IN DETROIT

Detroit, or at least its suburbs, was the last holdout. After all, the city was America's manufacturing capital and the top of the manufacturing food chain. The automobile was symbolic of the nation itself. No product contains such a variety of parts. Now, imported cars take a bite out of almost every American industry. The automobile is part of the fabric of American society. In the 1950s and 1960s, the purchase of a "chrome god" was the rite of passage into the American middle class. America in 1950 was supplying almost 80 percent of the world's cars; but by 1980, that share had dropped to 30 percent. In 1980, Detroit was willingly surrendering more domestic share as well. Detroit had coasted high on the 1978 auto boom, believing it could afford to surrender 22 percent of the market to imports by holding onto the larger, more profitable cars. In 1978 the American auto companies made 9.3 million cars. Detroit had stopped the newcomers in the early 1980s with Japanese voluntary constraints on imported cars. Detroit auto makers with "buy American campaigns" had slowed the Japanese penetration, all the time throwing the domestic parts suppliers under the bus by buying imported parts, tires, and steel. Now the wolf had come to the auto makers themselves.

The heart of the problem seemed to be in wages and productivity. From 1980 to 1990, American auto workers were making $19 an hour in wages and benefits compared to $12 an hour for the Japanese. The Japanese also had a 2 to 1 edge in robots. The Japanese produced twice as much with half the labor, at half the cost: that's some productivity gap.

The Japanese had superior technology, and some of their productivity advantage came from outsourcing labor to specialized suppliers. The newer Japanese equipment and plant expansion was made possible by American banking investments. Unfortunately, this was overlooked as American management and the unions blamed each other, and the government looked to retraining displaced workers and doubling down on free trade economics.

The "Japanese Miracle" did inspire managers, labor leaders, and politicians to make week-long trips to find out how they did it. The answers were endless, depending on the point someone wanted to make. We were told it was their statistical process control, employee teams, better employee treatment, better work ethic of the workers, their problem solving methods, and better management. A wave of Japanese methodology was implemented in American industry. Driven by Ford and General Motors, suppliers plastered walls with statistical control charts to improve quality audit results, based on the idea more was better. Most of these methods, like statistical process control, were overdone and showed little measurable results. Methodology became the focus in a misinterpretation of the Japanese mystery. In fact, the Japanese had few real secrets other than a passion to compete. The lean manufacturing of Toyota (originally from Henry Ford) did prove valuable, but widespread implementation in the US only came in the late 1990s. The productivity and cost advantages were real, however, in the 1980s and 1990s.

As early as the 1960s, top management in the Big Three auto makers was moving away from the practices of the old barons such as Henry Ford and Alfred Sloan. Operating executives were no longer favored for the key company positions. Money moved out of the plants as finance and marketing people took over running the companies. Henry Ford had put all his money in the plants, creating a better engineered car — albeit, one color and one design. Now auto makers searched for "better" uses of their capital.

American manufacturers made things worse by lowering quality, maintaining archaic marketing strategies, and using decentralized manufacturing. Quality failures might have been the worst self-inflicted wound in Detroit. The idea that it was better not to buy cars made on a Monday or Friday went from urban legend in the 1960s to a well-known reality in the 1970s. From 1975 to 1990, quality concerns were the fault of the auto makers (management and union), auto suppliers, and government. Relations with the supply chain and the government became adversarial.

The Detroit quality problem had surfaced in the early 1970s as General Motors challenged Japan with its Vega model, and Ford with its Pinto. As we have seen, the Lordstown-built Vega suffered from labor problems, but there were also design issues. The Vega had new technology in its aluminum engine block, which dramatically reduced weight, but the engine proved noisy and prone to overheating. Oil leaks were common as well. It created a poor image for American small cars as Japanese imports were surging.

Ford entered the small car market in the 1970s with its Pinto. The Pinto used a more conservative design than the Vega, but the Pinto had a flaw in its fuel filter design that could cause a fire in the event of a rear-end collision. Several deaths made national news, and Ford was charged with criminal reckless homicide. Ford stonewalled the fix, and it was costly. While this defect was the headliner, maybe in the long run a rust problem was more damaging to the car's reputation, and it was a problem well known to Pinto and Ford owners in general. The problem lay in Ford's painting and coating processes and the steel it purchased. Cars were literally rusting away at 50,000 miles. The rust problem eroded customer loyalty to Ford products. Still, consumers retained their loyalty to American companies.

Ford had remained the most loyal buyer of American steel, but now the rust problem opened a new door for Japanese steel. This created tension between domestic steel companies and Ford. The Japanese were making zinc-coated steel with superior corrosion resistance. Quality had been ignored too long by all of American industry. Both Ford and the steel makers knew the steel was a problem. One steel manager laughably admitted that the floor fell out of his Pinto while he was driving to work.

In the first decades after the war, "Made in Japan" had meant both cheap and poor quality. Now, the Japanese were gaining a notable reputation for good quality, but American consumers were slow to change their habits. First, routine maintenance for Japanese cars was not as easy, given the extensive dealership and independent repair network for American cars. Just as important was a love affair with big, heavy cars. The large, comfortable interior was one thing; the impressive exterior was another. And consumers often viewed the little foreign models as unsafe in crashes. This consumer loyalty would change quickly with the Oil Crisis of 1973. Gasoline prices, prior to the 1970s, had been a minor concern with the American consumer. Oil prices from 1948 to 1971 had been steady around $2 a barrel.

[please delete, or combine with earlier OPEC discussions]

The Arab Oil Embargo in 1973, described above, would mark the true beginning of the energy crisis. The American auto industry was caught off guard with large gas-guzzlers in their showrooms. Imported gas-efficient car sales surged; and even though the embargo lasted only six months, buying patterns were changed forever. At the end of the six-month embargo, oil would be $18 a barrel with daily movements as high as $22 a barrel. The shock of the embargo helped pass the trans-Alaska Pipeline in 1973 and expanded oil exploration. Mass transit projects, carpooling, and other conservation projects came into vogue. In addition, the 45 percent increase in fuel prices caused a worldwide recession and helped contribute to what would be called stagflation. These fuel costs rippled through the economy creating higher food costs and high inflation. The 1970s will always be remembered for this extraordinary spike of inflation, which hurt everyone. Most specifically, though, the Oil Embargo had its greatest effect on the automotive industry.

This was the beginning of the end of the popularity of big six-cylinder and V8 cars. Japanese four-cylinder cars such as Toyota Corona, Toyota Corolla, Honda Civic, and the Datsun 510 became popular. American manufacturers couldn't sell off their inventory of large cars and in those days it took up to four years to bring a new model to market. In addition, Datsun had just released its upscale 610 aimed at the high price market. The Big Three were forced to develop four-cylinder and smaller models such as the Ford Pinto, Chevy Vega, and Plymouth Valiant. Longer run, a number of energy acts were passed in Washington in the late 1970s to address conservation and energy usage. The Department of Energy was created in 1977. Still, the Big Three were quick to focus again on high-profit large cars when the crisis was over; but consumers by then had seen the benefit of smaller, fuel efficient cars, and that trend would only continue to increase. By 1975, the Japanese had secured an amazing 18 percent of the American market. Even so, American auto makers were content to give up small models and maintain their dominance in the high profit big models and up scale models.

The real revolution hit the market in 1976 with the Honda Accord. Honda was basically a motorcycle company that had not built its first car until 1962. The Honda Accord was a major advance in small car technology. Its overhead camshaft and aluminum engine were state of the art. The Honda put fear in the Detroit research centers.

The Honda Accord was like a German-engineered car with a Japanese price tag, in the midst of a major decline in American quality. It would win over youthful buyers and become an American favorite. A top automotive journalist observed, "Not since the upper middle class and the academic community took the Volkswagen Beetle to their hearts in the early 1950s had a small car enjoyed so much cachet. The Honda Accord was a brilliant amalgam of automotive philosophies and it was attracting an influential, upscale group of customers."[1] In addition, Honda exploited an American marketing weakness by selling a "complete" car without the long list of necessary but costly "options."

Winning over the affluent upper middle class was the last straw. The upper middle class was the mainstay of universities, government administration, college educated teachers, and professionals, all of which were immune to the direct impact of imports to the American economy. The upper middle class proved resistant to "Buy American" campaigns. Appalled by the Vietnam War, this group saw nothing patriotic in buying American; in fact, driving a foreign car made a political protest statement. The Honda Accord was a reasonable compromise between cost and driveway status like the Volkswagen Beetle. A fully packed small American J-car offered neither economy nor status. The Honda Accord made it OK to buy foreign for all the middle class. And the growing reputation for poor quality of American cars helped mitigate the social scorn that an Accord driver might feel in blue collar neighborhoods.

The government's role in reducing auto quality has, to a large degree, been lost to history. The Corporate Average Fuel Economy (CAFÉ) regulations played an important part, starting in 1976.[2] It had been preceded by the 1970 Clean Air Act that caught Detroit unprepared. CAFÉ was part of the government response to the environmental movement and fuel saving effort, but the timing hit the automakers in the worst period in their struggle against the imports and oil shortages. This government mandate forced American automakers to sell more small cars when they were not profitable and/or to reduce their car sizes and weights. The Japanese faced no real immediate changes because their product mix already included small cars. These same government regulations hit American consumers hard, too, in repair costs, but the auto companies were saddled with costs that would sink them in a number of ways.

These regulations were appropriate for a market and technology that at the time didn't exist. This caused a panic in Detroit. Detroit pushed to reduce car weight, even ignoring engineering needs to replace nuts and

---

1   Brock Yates, *The Decline & Fall of the American Automobile Industry*, (New York: Vintage Books, 1984), p. 42

2   Brock Yates, *The Decline & Fall of the American Automobile Industry*, (New York: Vintage Books, 1984), p. 237

bolts with welds or epoxy. Sheet metal thickness was reduced. Rejected steel from major mills might be purchased on the secondary market for use in cars. Price pressure on suppliers created an environment for lower quality as well. Lighter weight braces were used. The light weight unit body construction pioneered at Lordstown, to enable more automated welding, lacked the necessary structural strength. Government and the industry became adversarial instead of cooperative in facing these requirements.

After the 1973 Oil Crisis, the Big Three returned to business as usual. Union contacts were generously settled. At the beginning of the 1970s, auto workers made 30 percent more than the average industrial worker; and by the end of the seventies, 60 percent more. Supplemental Unemployment benefits were added, assuring the worker 95 percent of their pay for a year. It was so good that older workers wanted to be laid off first so they could enjoy hunting and fishing while collecting 95 percent of their pay. The problem was that these layoffs were becoming more frequent and lasting longer — with more never being called back.

Light cars required by the Clean Air Act and the oil prices changed the very infrastructure of the City of Detroit. Woodward Avenue was the heart and soul of the Motor City. In the morning it brought automotive executives from Detroit's best suburbs in their Bonneville and New Yorker cars to their offices. In the evening, the youth in their muscle cars cruised the endless avenue of diners and gasoline stations. Its wide lanes made it ideal for urban racing of Mustangs, Plymouth Road Runners, T-Birds, and Corvettes. Many executives looked to Woodward as a marketing test site. By the 1970s, the muscle cars were gone and Woodward, like Detroit, would show the destruction brought by de-industrialization. The changes on Woodward Avenue augured more changes in the automotive industry and Detroit in particular. By 1979, Japanese cars were appearing on Woodward Avenue.

As the recession of the 1980s sent millions of workers to the unemployment lines, the political battle heated up on the Japanese auto imports. Japan had over 20 percent of the American auto market but practiced protectionism in their own country. In hindsight, the war was probably over by the 1990s. The Mont Pèlerin economists had by now taken over the halls of American government. Still the UAW and other unions were a powerful force, and Japanese protectionism made it a target. American politicians crafted a system of voluntary constraints on imports. This was a protectionist move without making a philosophical commitment to American manufacturing. Pressure continued, but to a large degree, politicians on both sides stonewalled. There were "buy American" clauses placed in government contracts, but all these were far short of what was needed to save American manufacturing.

Japan countered by building auto plants in the United States. In the early 1980s, Honda had built its first auto plant in Marysville, Ohio. It continued to expand during the 1980s as Toyota followed. Building their plants in America allowed the Japanese companies to get around voluntary contracts while muting protectionist bills in Congress by hiring American employees. The Japanese companies favored southern Ohio and Indiana, and later the deeper South, in an effort to avoid UAW wages and benefits. The American production of Japanese cars broke down the barriers and resistance of pro-protectionists. The Japanese strategy played into the American political divide. The union's alliance with the Democrats now made it impossible to win over Republicans in right-to-work states winning Japanese plants. The political divide prevented any national-unity effort to stop the runaway train of de-industrialization of America. The latest generation of economists argued that this globalization would bring a new balance to American manufacturing, shifting much of it to the more competitive Southern labor. The loss of Northern auto related jobs would, however, far outpace the transplant jobs of the Japanese and Germans.

The United Autoworkers proved more flexible than other industrial unions in later years. Their bigger problem would become their one-party system. As with other unions, the singular link to the Democratic Party split politicians and consumers. Southern consumers had proven loyal to American auto purchasers, but the use of union money to fund opposition to their favorite Republican politicians created conflict. The split would widen in the 1990s as the non-union South developed an automotive industry of foreign transplant companies from Japan and Germany. Bills to support American auto producers now found Southern Republican opposition just when alliances were most needed.

The great recession of the early 1980s also started a new trend among manufacturers to counter the success autoworkers had experienced in wage advances during the 1970s. Auto companies and suppliers looked to reduce the $20 an hour UAW wage to $12 an hour in the non-union South and Mexico, and even further to $3 an hour by outsourcing to Korea. Other American industries moved to Korea, too, in the 1980s. Not only did the Koreans work for a low wage, but they put in 12 hour days, six days a week. Out of this great Korean movement came the rise of

Hyundai Motors, which decades later would deal another crushing blow to American automakers.

How far has the "creative destruction" of de-industrialization taken Detroit? In 1954, Detroit had the highest per capita income and the highest home ownership in the United States. Now it ranks lowest. In its peak in the 1960s, Detroit had over 290,000 manufacturing jobs; now it has fewer than 27,000. Even in the first few years of the 2000s, the Detroit area lost another 150,000 auto jobs. Crime has gotten so bad the police barely try to deal with most of it. Homicides hit 386 in 2012, and 90 percent of the crimes go unsolved. Some neighborhoods are too dangerous for even police patrols. Drug dealers find the area dangerous, too. It is more dangerous for Americans than in our war zones. Over 50 percent of the city's children are classified as poor and illiterate. Less than 40 percent graduate from high school, and even those who do can barely read. The infant mortality rate of 16 per thousand is higher than in the Dominican Republic. Over 40 percent of the city's street lights don't work; most have been stripped of their copper wiring for drug money. Old houses are fire wood for the homeless. The city is $12 billion in debt and has halted most road and sidewalk repair. Over 30 percent of the ambulances and emergency vehicles don't run. The police response time averages 58 minutes; they have red lined certain neighborhoods as too dangerous for response. The crime rate is five times that of New York City. Real unemployment is around 50 percent. Over 30 percent of the buildings are vacant. Many houses are selling for under $500.

The median house price is $6,000. Often only a single house per block has a living occupant. It's hard to sleep in the downtown hotels, as the night sounds of sirens and gun fire continue until day break. Many state residents will not even drive near Detroit after sunset. City blocks have started to revert to woodlands. Politicians are actually promoting farming in downtown Detroit. Detroit residents have been "retrained," using billions of tax dollars, for decades, for a non-existent future. In their worst days, the industrial "bad" neighborhoods of Detroit were Edens compared to today's de-industrialized neighborhoods. Without welfare support, Detroit lacks a stable income source and barely has the infrastructure necessary for people to live. Detroit has become a ward of the State of Michigan and Washington DC. Politicians have tried everything short of calling back the Roman Emperor Nero to burn it down. Yet no one points to US economic policy as the reason for this decline. Can anyone really believe you can re-build Detroit without industry? For residents of Detroit who can remember them, the Depression years of the 1930s were good times. Billions of US tax dollars are spent to rebuild other countries, while Detroit dies. Even our churches don't understand how devastated the cities are. Churches continue to send missionaries to "poor" countries as our cities are ignored. Most of these "poor" countries are better off than Detroit.

The illiterate, homeless, poor, and unemployed cannot enjoy the promised benefits of cheaper costs of living brought by free trade. The Detroit area is too depressed to attract new Wal-Marts. Without money or anything of value left to trade for drugs, even gangs are leaving. Reasons, like solutions, are attributed to everything except de-industrialization via economic policy.

The greater worry is that Detroit is playing out the future of many American cities as de-industrialization spreads. De-industrialization is more like a black hole than a cancer, sucking in the rest of the country. We worry about the national debt, arguing over tax increases or government program cuts, ignoring the possible solution of re-building industry in America. We pour endless funds into schemes to protect national and homeland security, while even the military sees our declining economy as the bigger threat to our security.

In July of 2013, Detroit filed for bankruptcy, crushed by the unsecured debt owed to union public employees. Like most cities during the great American prosperity, over extended wages and benefits were owed to public employees. The unions resisted any settlement to reduce pensions and health care coverage, unlike the United Auto Workers a decade earlier. Detroit learned the hard way that increasing the tax base by taxing working people more only accelerates the decline. What is needed is an expanded tax base from industry. Detroit was a once great city; stripped of its industry, it is left with an unaffordable city infrastructure.

Many Americans seem to accept the development of economic wastelands like Detroit, Akron, South Chicago, and Youngstown; they still see Detroit and other rust belt cities as isolated cases. More and more Americans have come to accept industrial decline and national decline. We have come to believe that capitalism requires free trade and less prosperity for America, believing that the destruction will pass over our houses.

Most Americans accept that they will make less than their parents. De-industrialization has not only stripped us of the American dream but our own individual dreams. Americans give generously to poor nations, which are far better off than then many of our major cities. Now these Third World countries are sending their priests and ministers to do missionary service in America. We protest the killing that results from war when a soldier is more likely to die from gunfire during a visit home in our cities. We worry about global warming while our cities burn. We talk of trade wars hurting our economy, not realizing the war is over, and we lost. De-industrialization seems unstoppable. The homeless, unemployed, illiterate, and uneducated have become the hopeless. We are promised that industry is not needed: that the solution is retraining, green jobs, expanded safety nets, more taxes, improved race relations, more international trade, more high tech, less protectionism, more casinos, more community colleges, and so on. Many believe that it simply boils down to which political party is in control. Every American should have to spend a week in Detroit to fully understand the impact of de-industrialization.

CHAPTER 13. DE-INDUSTRIALIZATION OF AN AMERICAN COMPANY — JONES & LAUGHLIN (AKA LTV)

De-industrialization stripped communities and individuals of their identity. Part of that identity was with the companies these individuals worked for. It may seem strange to people in Washington DC and to non-industrial employees, but companies are mourned too. It's natural for employees to proudly identify with great corporations that employ them, fund cultural events in their cities, and contribute the bulk of the taxes that support municipal services. Companies are made up of people and they have hearts and souls, which is reflected in their culture and history. The story of LTV Steel (the remnants of Jones & Laughlin Steel, Youngstown Steel, and Republic Steel) reflects the rise, decline, and fall of American industry on a different level. It is a personal level. It is a different perspective that colors the view of de-industrialization. The demise of a company is often mourned by employees and community.

There were few tears shed for LTV Steel, but its heart was the old Jones & Laughlin Steel that even predated Carnegie in Pittsburgh. J&L Pittsburgh Works (Southside) was the only steel mill inside the city limits of Pittsburgh. United States Steel formed a ring around Pittsburgh. Furthermore, Jones & Laughlin predated the Carnegie organization by more than 25 years. Jones & Laughlin's iconic Eliza Furnaces were the only blast furnaces one saw when traveling the expressways through the city.

Pittsburgh's first "Iron Baron," Benjamin Jones, was the founder of J & L Steel; he was later joined by James Laughlin. His first iron making operation in Pittsburgh continued to produce iron from 1851 to 1983. The early iron works prospered under the protectionist trade policies of Abraham Lincoln. This continued with a succession of protectionist Republican presidents and congressmen. The Pittsburgh Works were fundamental to American industry in the 1870s. It would be Benjamin Jones that Andrew Carnegie came to admire as a young telegraph boy. Jones was bigger than life, and he made the iron industry a source of wealth and pride for many. Jones would become a major financial supporter for protectionist policies and the Republican Party. He built loyal organizations at the mill as well. Jones & Laughlin were dedicated to improving steel making technology and expanding employment. The company, however, would fall in the 1970s to de-industrialization. In an effort to return it to profitability, it was purchased by turnaround specialists LTV Corporation.

LTV would prove more adept at corporate culture busting than steelmaking. LTV was typical of the worst of management mistakes in the steel business at its most critical period. In defense of LTV, it was working with the assumption that the problem with steel lay in the history of poor management and labor relations. It had no concept that the discussions by a certain elite on a Swiss mountain a few decades earlier were the real problem; and the wave of American de-industrialization could not be stopped by greater cooperation within the corporations. Yes, this new global world had exposed some structural problems in many companies, but no one could compete against imported steel being sold at prices below the cost of raw materials. Still, LTV took on management and labor relations with the zeal of a crusader. LTV believed that the old time steel managers lacked the guts to make the necessary tough decisions. In making tough decisions, LTV would prove to be as cold and hard as the steel they made.

LTV represented a change that took from Jones & Laughlin Steel's heart and soul. It stripped the company of its history, culture, and its relationship with the community. It was an example of how steel and other industries had become merely businesses. Still, it was said to be necessary in an effort to meet global market prices. Where once the boys of Carnegie talked steelmaking over Monongahela rye whiskey late into the night at the famous Duquesne Club, this new breed of the 1970s discussed balance sheets over fine imported wine. Once a new blast furnace was a source of pride and awe in dinner conversations; stock investments seemed more exciting now. These new managers found no pride in managing steel but saw it as just a commodity. They believed a good manager could manage in any industry without a relationship with the industry itself. They saw no need for a bond with the community, just a business relationship.

LTV had a culture, but it was one of investment bankers, which was imposed on the steel companies it acquired. Jones & Laughlin managers had tended to be industry savvy and technical. Metallurgical backgrounds were highly prized. The managers were hands on, short-sleeved types. They tended to have a deeper allegiance to their mill than to the company as a whole. They loved the history and the tradition. They loved the long hours of a 24/7 operation. They were proud of their work. To reach the level of assistant superintendent or superintendent of a mill was a proud career moment for them and their family. Sadly, their time was over. This type of manager was ill suited for the endless and heartless cutting that was required.

LTV's history was of buying companies and turning them around started from the original company of James J. Ling. This was the Dallas-based Ling Electric in 1947. LTV expanded into electronics and missiles, buying Temco in 1961. The next year it added Vought Aircraft to become LTV formally in 1974. In 1962, LTV was number 244 on the Fortune 500. The company was not only in electronics and aircraft, but insurance, banking, car rental, and an airline. LTV was the darling of the stock market following the conglomerate model of ITT. The model included the idea of the universal manager capable of managing any organization regardless of product. James Ling had gained a reputation of a turnaround wizard.

His 1968 purchase of J & L Steel would be his Waterloo; and it cost him his personal fortune. What Ling saw was a turnaround opportunity and a mountain of cash in J & L's pension funds. Ling and his young team believed they could change the course of the steel industry. LTV managers made tough business decisions, alright, and mistakes. However, it would be an injustice to consider them villains. In the bigger picture, this was all part of the process of de-industrialization.

Jones & Laughlin managers, as noted, were steel men first and foremost. In the late 1950s and early 1960s, Jones & Laughlin invested in new technology, pioneering Basic Oxygen Furnaces and Continuous Casters at its Aliquippa and Cleveland mills. It added a blast furnace at its Cleveland Works to make it one of the world's most modern in the 1960s. But then things changed. The 1963 political pressure of the Kennedy Administration to hold steel prices was a setback for the company. Soon both the market imports and market prices were being set by the government. They couldn't earn back the investment they'd made in their own plant under these conditions; no wonder a decade later Tom Graham of United States Steel (on the J & L team in the 1960s) decided to invest in Marathon Oil versus plant expansion. Men of steel no longer desired to be in the industry. To a degree, they no longer were able to, because the boards of these failing companies were demanding a return to profitability.

This meant that operating changes had to be made. The deal with LTV had some provisions to prevent the burning and salting of J & L management. Ling, however, clearly set the tone of what a LTV manager was to be like. Ling had been successful with many smaller companies, but heavy industry would prove far different than lighter manufacturing. The first changes seemed subtle enough; titles such as foreman were changed to supervisor. Manager was preferred over superintendent. LTV would never fully realize what an important and integral part of the culture titles represented. Chief Metallurgist titles were replaced with manager. It was a message that managers were above product knowledge or product experience and a different skill set was preferred. It was typical of LTV which tried to change culture through organizational philosophy. LTV injected lawyers into its employee services and personnel departments. It reveled in putting women into manager positions, not to increase gender equality but to send a message that a manager was not the typical "steelworker." Unfortunately, this was a misguided strategy, since in hindsight management and the workers were not the problems.

LTV felt it had to change the typical steel manager. It had an informal rule that its managers wear long-sleeve shirts (preferably white or blue, no stripes). Managers who refused to conform to these informal dress codes limited their careers. Blue pin-striped suits were preferred for business meetings. Managers were to wear suits distinguishing them from the hands-on, down and dirty management style of old steel managers. One LTV manager at Pittsburgh Works wore a white suit to show he managed the melt shop through his frontline supervisors, not his direct supervision. To wear a white suit in the dirtiest of operations was a statement of non-hands on. He further removed himself from the traditional role of melt shop supervision; that fast tracked his career at LTV. This was part of the LTV conversion strategy. Instead of mass firings, managers who embraced the LTV philosophy were fast tracked. Managers were to be removed from the daily front lines, and they were not allowed to wear beepers. Knowledge of steelmaking took a back seat to management training. Liberal arts majors were preferred over engineers and metallurgists to manage the operation. The approach was not without its benefits, but it strips an industry as well as the employee of their uniqueness. This was a dramatic change after over a hundred years of tradition.

Bringing in LTV was like the highly paid successful football coach brought in to run the Ohio State or Michigan football program without understanding the tradition; they were doomed to failure even on a level playing field. In industries like steel, rubber, and auto companies, tradition is more important than most managers think. People are proud to be part of the tradition; it separates them from being a generic worker. Workers' wardrobes always consisted of their Steelers jacket, and their J&L jacket for more formal events. Workers knew the company history as well as the plant history. At Halloween, there were always rewrites of the ghost stories related to J&L's Pittsburgh Works in the newspapers. LTV believed this strong steel culture got in the way of profitable management in tough times.

LTV labeled the traditional Industrial Engineering departments as archaic and unnecessary and gutted them. It adopted team manning, reducing former supervisors to team leaders or coordinators. This struck many proud foremen as a demotion. Technical people in areas like quality control were replaced with the new breed of generic manager. Staff organizations were eliminated wherever possible. Old organizational ties were destroyed. Over and over, they cut employees and then made things worse by a sweeping reorganization of those who remained. Employees, managers, and the union had to deal with constant organizational change.

LTV were right about one thing in the steel industry organization; the history of fighting between management and the union had to stop. Internal conflicts could not be afforded in the global market. Employee improvement teams became an obsession with LTV. The teams became power bases in themselves, threatening the union and frontline supervisors. In addition, the union was suspicious of management dealing directly with workers in cost reductions. LTV had some excellent approaches, but it lacked any sensitivity in implementing them in a culture well over a century old. Union was suspicious of cooperative approaches after decades of combat and even efforts of forming "company" unions. With time, LTV might have been successful, but the company and the industry were out of time.

Physically, LTV looked to rationalize the operations and infuse new technology and investment. At the time, Jones & Laughlin consisted of the two integrated mills in Pittsburgh and Aliquippa. Pittsburgh Works Southside was the oldest steel mill in the nation. LTV would tear down its famous five blast furnaces and the open hearth shop while starting two of the world's largest electric furnaces in 1979. The plan was to build a state of the art continuous strip caster. The great steel recession of 1982 would end that dream and spelled the beginning of the end of LTV Steel. Prior to 1982, LTV did upgrade its Aliquippa Works, but times were already changing.

LTV didn't wait, either; they were continually looking to buy or merge to strengthen the company. In 1978, LTV Jones & Laughlin purchased Youngstown Steel and Tube, which still had a fully integrated mill in Chicago and parts of finishing operations in Youngstown. With government resistance, it wasn't until 1981 that the formal merger of operations occurred. LTV had become the nation's third largest steel company. Youngstown Sheet & Tube offered some combined efficiencies by closing down redundant operations, but it also put massive loads of pensioners on the books. LTV looked for Japanese help in making the merger successful.

LTV Steel addressed its weakness in competitive technology by signing a major consulting and technology transfer contact with Sumitomo Steel of Japan, which would inspire other steel companies to do the same. The Japanese studied LTV for over $20 million. The final product was 10 large hard bound books with the LTV Jones & Laughlin name misspelled. It contained little new data and avoided the hard issues as seen by middle steel managers. LTV management made it a religion to ensure that all the suggestions were implemented. Most middle managers felt that the Japanese had learned more than they gave. Clearly, the market information gained by the Japanese was their main objective.

The merger of LTV Steel and Republic Steel in 1984 was a final effort to save yet another dying company and one near death. In normal times, LTV probably would have been successful. The combination offered lots of savings. It, however, would not address the labor costs and the dumping of imported steel. The company was able to cut salaried labor, but the morale issues proved even more damaging. Imported steel was flowing in from Brazil and Russia. The price below the materials costs of LTV, making it a "no-brainer" for LTV to purchase semi-finished and use its domestic rolling mills to make competitive product. The union, of course, objected, seeing the loss of jobs in the hot end of steelmaking. The problem was, both management and the union were right. This situation required protection of tariffs, but now even the US government's hands were tied with a maze of informal and formal free trade agreements. The Mont Pèlerin type trade controls and international machinery had taken away the US government's ability to move quickly. International political concerns trumped national concerns. The move to purchase semi-finished, cheap steel by the steel companies within two years crushed the hot end of steelmaking in the United States. Union and management became mired in a conflict that was actually being driven by outside forces. The culture that needed to be changed was that of international free trade. Still corporate culture was the only factor that management could change.

If LTV thought the culture conversion of Jones & Laughlin and Youngstown Sheet had been challenging, they ran into open rebellion with the acquisition of Republic Steel. Republic Steel was really a loose confederacy of individual steel mills in Cleveland, Canton, Massillon, Chicago and Warren. These mills were fiercely proud and competitive within the company. Plants like Chicago and Canton wouldn't even share company patents and special processing between plants. The Chicago plant even threatened the Canton plant with infringing on tool steel patents of the same company. Republic Steel's organization was designed for the American-dominant steel industry of an earlier century. The internal competition of Andrew Carnegie that was so successful in steel's glory days was now self-destructing in the new global steel industry. In fairness, Republic Steel needed to change, but LTV failed to manage that conversion. LTV had seen Jones & Laughlin's managers as a challenge, but they viewed Republic Steel managers with distain. Republic represented to them all that was wrong with American steel. Republic managers saw their LTV bosses as ignorant of the steelmaking process, as cold hearted, and as job cutting barbarians.

LTV, sadly, was right; not because Republic managers were poor managers, but the industry could no longer follow an operating philosophy based on domestic competition. The change would be hard on Republic managers. It had been fun and satisfying to be a steel manager at Republic. Steel metallurgy and technology expertise were prized. The Works Manager, like in the days of Carnegie, was feudal lord in the Republic Steel organization. Individual department superintendents approached the same level. There were country club memberships and meetings for them. The works manager had a large discretionary fund for community events. LTV saw these as "slush" funds. Superintendents had their own dining hall, like Jones & Laughlin before LTV. LTV lost no time closing down the dining hall. The company argued that it was aristocratic, but they missed the point of tradition and motivation. Of course, to the outsider, such dining halls may seem like a waste of money, but originally, the idea was to bring managers together at lunch to talk business. The works manager often made important announcements and it allowed for a daily exchange of ideas. Consider today that Google has over 20 specialty restaurants on site to promote work and interchange of ideas.

Sometimes this culture advanced too far. At Weirton Steel, there were once three dining halls for various levels of management, and it was even common to get a promotion in dining halls with no change in title or money. The lowest level management dining hall was served family-style by waitresses with no table cloth. The next level had a restricted but varied menu with individual service. Finally, the third dining "hall" had special linen, china, and silverware and the ability to special order. At least, the Republic dining halls did not discriminate among management. All this culture change, however, took up all the energy, so badly needed in the global market competition.

Feeling the need to move fast, LTV did not allow Republic three years to resist culture change as it had with Jones & Laughlin. Republic had to be assimilated quickly into the new culture. While LTV used all the "best" practices to facilitate the merger and assimilation, they lacked the personal touch. Jones & Laughlin managers were told that the LTV system was going in regardless of any public statements about Republic. At the time, LTV headquarters were moving to Cleveland, in the Republic Steel Building, and to the president of Republic Steel it looked as if maybe Republic was on even footing. Incoming LTV/Jones & Laughlin managers, who knew different, came in with an air of superiority. Eventually, all the Jones & Laughlin mills would be closed, and the LTV/ Jones & Laughlin managers would replace those in Republic's home mills. Dining halls and country club memberships were gone.

The bones and fossils of LTV are not just in Pittsburgh, Cleveland, Canton, and Youngstown. Maybe the true dinosaur of the LTV Museum is the town of Aliquippa, Pennsylvania, twenty miles down the Ohio River from Pittsburgh. Aliquippa was a steel town created by Jones and Laughlin Steel in 1905. Aliquippa grew from 620 people to a peak of 26,369 in 1957. J&L Aliquippa Works employed 15,000 that year. Aliquippa had a long history and the mill invested heavily in new technology after World War Two. It was a bustling community of middle class blue collar workers. Its blue star displayed on the blast furnace would represent the beginning of the Christmas season for those in the Ohio Valley.

In 1969, LTV took over the mill and major technology advances slowed. LTV Steel, in its defense, had purchased a number of internationally uncompetitive steel companies and was trying to rationalize operations. The anchor forged at Mont Pèlerin was dragging down the industry; the low cost of foreign labor far outweighed any possible technology enhancements; Aliquippa had a BOF, modern blast furnaces, and a continuous caster at the start of the 1970s. The union had made concessions and joined management in employee improvement teams. By 1984, Aliquippa was a marginal plant with the LTV takeover of Republic Steel. The plant struggled for a few years, but it was a losing cause. There was nothing more to give.

LTV's management became an easy target to take the blame, though some looked to the union. The government avoided any blame by rushing in with extended unemployment benefits and the usual political speeches blaming the other political party. These extended benefits did little to enable the workers to leave town. Aliquippa was steel, and there were no other steel companies for employment. There was nothing left for the town and its citizens.

The town was bankrupt, with Duquesne Light Company threatening to cut power for street lights. The forced retirements and plant closing payouts sent the oldest workers packing for Florida as the city effectively closed down. Aliquippa's population fell to under 10,000. The final statement by steelworkers came when the workers took over the iconic tunnels that led to the old plant. These "Tunnel Rats" were retirees who had lost their benefits with the 1987 bankruptcy of LTV Steel. The local police, with tears in their eyes, dragged out the retirees, charging them with disorderly conduct. By 1989, Aliquippa was completely shut down. Business had also declined through the eighties.

For sure, LTV had made some cold business decisions and often lacked heart, but Aliquippa's death warrant had been signed in 1947. Of course, the mill workers leaving the mill for the last time had never heard of Mont Pèlerin. Anger radiated in all directions except toward the originators of the political policy and the economic theories used to support it.

Chapter 14. Mont Pèlerin's Camelot in the 1990s

The dreams of the Mont Pèlerin group of European economists seemed centuries away in 1947, but the political environment and world socialism supplied the force to achieve nearly all the goals in 50 years. The victory in academia came within a few years far ahead of anyone's prediction. Mont Pèlerin Society meshed perfectly into the United Nations and world peace movement. They had envisioned the support of international bankers but believed national politics would slow the drive. How would bankers and politicians overcome the natural nationalism of workers in their individual countries? Initially, America was more than willing to share their wealth for world peace, realizing some workers would be displaced. Men like President John F. Kennedy knew that adjustment payments and retraining would be needed for displaced workers. Social movements in the West also played into de-industrialization. America's scars from Vietnam would make a new generation look differently at the hard work of the previous generation. This had surfaced at the highly automated Lordstown auto plant to meet Japanese competition.

The 1990s was the triumph of free trade arrangements such as NAFTA and the establishment of the World Trade Organization (WTO); these seemed little threat to the powerful unions in the United States. The World Trade Organization, which is an international organization to monitor trade disputes between nations, had also seemed unlikely to have been given so much power over nations. The WTO replaced the General Agreement on Tariffs and Trade (GATT) which was implemented by the Western nations after World War II to regulate trade and assure the world economic recovery in 1947. But under Democrat and Republican administrations alike, it rose to the level of one of the most powerful international organizations. The WTO makes it decisions on economics, not differences of labor and freedom.

As described above, many new technologies evolved in the 1980s and 1990s that also accelerated the downfall of American industry. Steel belted tires required completely new factories and high capital investment, at a time when American industry could least afford to make expensive technology changes. In steel, there was also a new technology that helped make the massive complex steel centers of World War II obsolete.

Steel mini mills were the last straw. Like the steel belted radial in the rubber industry, it would be foreign investors that seized the advantage. Mini-mills melted steel scrap in electric furnaces, far more efficiently than the high cost of smelting iron ore in massive blast furnaces. Mini-mills no longer required the extensive supply and transportation systems needed for iron ore and coal. The environmental nightmares of coke plants needed to prepare coal for use in the blast furnaces was eliminated. The reduction in hot metal costs was around $130 a ton for the mini-mills, about a 30 percent cost advantage over the big integrated mills. In the lower quality products, mini-mill and imports crushed the big integrated producers in the 1980s. By the 1990s, mini-mills had moved successfully into the high products as well as flat rolled automotive sheet.

In the first two years of the new century, seventeen domestic steel companies filed for bankruptcy including the behemoth Bethlehem Steel. The American era of steel was over. The gates of the mills in Pittsburgh, Youngstown, Bethlehem, and Cleveland, which had annually seen politicians handing out campaign literature, were long gone. The Democratic Party, which had been the backbone of the United States Steelworkers, had long ago deserted as the money and steelworker membership declined. The Steel Caucus in Congress was now history. Politicians don't like losers, especially those short on money and members who can vote. The government unions now had the seats of power once held by the steelworkers and rubber workers.

America's best economists, now followers of the Mont Pèlerin Society, offered answers to the questions of why America had not reaped the great prosperity promised by free trade. The problem lay with both unions and management, in their opinion. The nation that was no longer competitive. Unions were overpaid and inflexible, and management lacked creativity. American quality had fallen to the lowest level in the industrial West. American workers were lazy and lacked craftsmanship. Almost every reason was promoted with the exception that free trade was really a policy to promote American de-industrialization. America had fallen to the most powerful of imports — Austrian economics.

American manufacturers and the unions did not sit idle and watch this happen. They cut special deals to experiment with workplace issues. Companies sent an army of executives and engineers to study the success of the Japanese in the 1980s. Billions were spent by American industry in the 1980s and 1990s to re-establish American quality and reduce manufacturing costs. Millions were spent in technology exchanges, Japanese consultants, and joint ventures to make America competitive. But still, foreign workers had few benefits and worked for low wages, and competing countries had protective policies. The playing field was never level under Mont Pèlerin free trade economics. This was a re-distribution of global wealth, through trade, out of the United States. America was trying to play with a stacked deck in the 1990s.

Nor was American management sleeping, as many claimed. While the de-industrialization of America had many complex factors such as the dollar policy, aging manufacturing plants, post-war over capacity, trade deficit, union wage and benefit demands, the decline in manufacturing quality was one of the more controllable factors at the plant level. The decline of quality in American manufacturing became obvious in the 1970s. The high comparative quality of the Japanese imports accelerated the loss of market share to small Japanese cars. The competitive losses launched a decade of soul searching. In 1980, an NBC television program entitled "If Japan Can . . . Why Can't We?" started that process. The show highlighted W. Edwards Deming as a quality guru with some answers, or at least suggestions. His popularity grew; and in 1986, Deming published his own answer in *Out of the Crisis*. The result was a massive quality movement in the United States that in the next several years restored much of the lost quality. Today, American cars have finally reached world-class quality levels again.

W. Edwards Deming had worked with Walter Shewhart at Western Electric in the application of statistical process control. Shewhart had published the first industrial use of statistical process control in his work, *Economic Control of Quality Manufactured Product*, in 1931. Deming went on to applied statistics to his work at the census bureau; and during World War II, Deming trained American manufacturers in the quality production of war materials. After the war, Deming was assigned to several projects in the rebuilding of Japan. He gained popularity with a series of lectures to the Union of Japanese Scientists and Engineers (JUSE). Deming was part of a movement to make Japanese industry world competitive. While much credit is given to Deming's statistical techniques, the real power of Deming's approach lies in its focused goal of improvement that matched the national goal of reviving Japan as an economic power. Japan's success became equated with Deming and his statistical process control.

Deming believed the quality problems were largely related to the focus on mass production. Quantity became the goal and focus of mass production, with an entropic decline. Deming took to task American management. As part of the solution, Deming argued for the implementation of objective evaluations using statistical process control (SPC). To some degree, these statistical methods were a logical improvement of Fredrick Taylor's ideas of scientific management. American management tended to ignore Deming's other emphasis: on worker involvement. Statistical process control became the Holy Grail of the auto industry and its suppliers in the 1980s.

The Japanese manufacturing miracle by the 1970s spurred American companies to try the new approach. The ideas of Deming became popular in the country of origin in the 1980s. Deming would become a consultant for organizations such as Ford Motor, General Motors, and the Department of Defense. Some original Japanese ideas on employee teams ('quality circles' in Japan) were added and refined. But it was too late for some 37 million industrial workers who lost jobs in the 1970s and 1980s.[1]

Under cost pressure and declining market share, the American automotive industry was dragged into new quality initiatives such as Ford Q1, General Motors' Targets of Excellence, and Chrysler's Penstar program. These programs adopted statistical process control as their core. Auto suppliers wallpapered factories with statistical control charts that did little except make the auto company auditors happy. During the 1980s and 1990s, the government poured educational money into statistical training and so did companies. It was a sincere but misguided effort. Consultants got rich with the new movement, but American manufacturing companies gained little against their global competitors. In fairness, the constant cost pressure in the auto supply chain offered little opportunity to test quality programs anyway.

---

1 "Employment in NonFarm Payrolls by Major Industrial Sectors," Department of Labor, Bureau of Labor Statistics, 2008

Deming's ideas of the quality process were incorporated in the international manufacturing standard of ISO 9000. ISO 9000 forced companies to standardize processes much as Fredrick Taylor had standardized products in the twentieth century. ISO 9000 also added a system approach, forcing companies to use a systematic and documented approach to problem solving. The ISO concept came from Europe and contrasted with the Deming's statistical approach. The automotive companies, wanting a stronger emphasis on statistics and specific customer requirements, created additional requirements to ISO 9000, calling the standard QS 9000 in 1990. A new generation of consultants and government handouts continued with little change in the global auto market. Today the automotive version is known as TS 16949, but the statistical core has been dropped.

The United States also recognized the need for national quality examples; and in 1987, it established the Malcolm Baldridge Award to highlight America's best example of quality manufacturing and service each year. In the 1960s, Japan had implemented the Deming Award to honor quality performance. The Reagan Administration believed we needed a similar emphasis on a national level. Some early winners of the Baldridge Award included Motorola, Westinghouse Electric, and Xerox.

The quality movement of the 1980s and 1990s did help restore American quality, but it could not eliminate the impact of the economic factors driving American de-industrialization. The Baldridge winning programs of General Electric and Motorola morphed into the use of experimental design and statistical methods in their "six sigma" program for employee problem-solving teams. Six Sigma included the cost of quality, which Genichi Taguchi had made popular in the 1990s. Six Sigma programs combine statistical tools to allow employee teams to analyze process performance and design experiments to improve the process. Today the Baldridge Award has been defunded (a process that started in 2004). With its emphasis on employee problem-solving, Six Sigma is the lone survivor of the great statistical process control movement of the 1980s. These programs failed in the short run, but not without a real effort by American management to do something to turn things around. Management, also to their credit, tried to increase employee input with new workplace factories such as General Motors' Saturn. Quality in the auto industry was improved by the new focus, but the cost problems remain.

Auto management hardly stood still as many claim; it tried new approaches to reduce costs. General Motors in the 1990s aggressively attacked the high costs of auto parts. General Motors CEO Roger Smith promoted Inaki Lopez from its European operations to become corporate purchasing czar. Lopez's simple mission was to take major costs out of building cars. Lopez would become the scourge of the auto supply chain. He made suppliers bid against each other, rejecting bids to force additional bids lower. With some suppliers, he might just declare they should reduce their prices by 10 percent if they wanted the General Motors business. He sent teams of efficiency experts to suppliers' plants to find how they could achieve savings and then demanded half the "savings" be taken off the price. Operations savings program were forced on suppliers as a means to lower prices.

In the end, Lopez saved General Motors billions of dollars; but in doing so, he destroyed the American auto supply chain. Many saw Lopez as making the suppliers pay for General Motors' inefficiency. Most suppliers saw Lopez's untraditional approach as unethical. Suppliers who won the business often were in bankruptcy court by the end of the decade. General Motors would survive another decade. The Lopez "experiment" tested further the myth that the cost problems were in manufacturing, not in politics. The Mont Pèlerin Society had succeeded in making it taboo to blame anything on "free trade." No one of any intelligence could possibly be a trade protectionist according to their dismissal strategy. The economic press and politicians continued their tirades over the failure of American managers and workers. The industry itself seemed to believe the only hope was to drive costs below world prices. General Motors' was undaunted by its earlier small car failures. The new Saturn division tried to further address cost, quality, and manufacturing.

CHAPTER 15. WHO KILLED SATURN?

General Motors had attempted to take on the Japanese in the 1970s with technology at its Lordstown plant. Its failure was rooted in labor relations and marketing. General Motors would try to take on the Japanese imports again in 1985. This time they would build a state of art factory and support it with revolutionary labor relationships and marketing. It was the brainchild of General Motors Chairman Roger Smith, but this time the very structure and organization would be designed jointly by General Motors management and the United Autoworkers. For Roger Smith, "Saturn became not just a company but a cause."[1]

The proposed Saturn Corporation would address the criticisms that management and the union were doing nothing right. Economists, who held to their theory that free trade was best, had criticized American industry for its failure to compete with imports. In February of 1984, an historic "Group of 99" was established to make Saturn Corporation (a wholly owned subsidiary) operational. The 99 was composed of managers, staff, and union representatives from 17 General Motors divisions and 14 UAW regions. Manufacturing would be at Spring Hill, Tennessee (45 miles south of Nashville) but would be represented by the United Autoworkers (UAW). It would be a unique, innovative, and experimental partnership for the union and management. Saturn would function as a separate company with its own sales and marketing.

---

1 Paul Ingrassia, "Saturn Couldn't Escape GM's Dysfunctional Orbit," *Wall Street Journal*, October 2, 2009

The selection of Spring Hill was to get as far away as possible from the old operating paradigms of Detroit. General Motors, however, felt that it would be a bridge too far to go non-union as the Japanese transplants had done in Southern states. Particularly, such a move could complicate relationships with the union at other plants. The wages were set at 80 percent of standard UAW wages. Workers would be called "technicians," which was meant to reflect their flexible use in the work place. The workers still had the UAW benefits package. In reality, Saturn workers were still operating at 40 percent higher labor costs than foreign competitors and non-union plants. The UAW did agree to flexible jobs, which help eliminate union work rule costs, and which were estimated at $300 to $500 per union built car. All workers would be "technicians" with pay based on acquired skills. In traditional auto plants, if the assembly broke down, the operating workers would sit back as maintenance workers came in. With Saturn, operating workers might help out doing low end maintenance jobs. The agreement, while noncompetitive with Japanese auto workers, was a big step for the UAW. Saturn workers did have a profit sharing clause, which it was hoped would boost overall pay.

Saturn could not break away from the traditional mindset. GM's CEO Roger Smith and UAW leadership made an honest effort to change automotive culture, but middle management and middle union leadership lacked the same commitment. Things had not really changed in the auto industry. The changed marketing and sales strategy were innovative as was the unionized work environment. However, the fixed price, no-haggle sales approach, and no-haggle service strategy, never really caught on with the consumer as predicted.

The first Saturn product to come to market in 1990 had innovative parts such as plastic panels, but most of the engineering was that of GM's compacts. Saturn was made to appear as a new company, but in reality it was a division. The new "favored" division generated jealousy from the Chevy Division.[1]

There is some question whether Saturn ever was profitable. The real problem, however, was never sales, marketing, or even engineering. The problem was cost and low productivity. The effort to improve operations through partnership never succeeded. The union never fully trusted management, and the model slowly eroded. The original partnership deteriorated. Finally, the union returned to a traditional contract in 1994. It wasn't all union either; GM management distributed corpo-

1 Alex Taylor, *Sixty to Zero: An Inside Look at the Collapse of General Motors and the Detroit Auto Industry*, New Haven: Yale University Press, 2010, p. 85

rate overhead to Saturn as well, taking profits away. It wasn't the workers, either. Japanese transplant factories in the United States have been globally competitive, using American workers. Their success is rooted in non-union workers, reduced health insurance, and 401K's in place of pensions. The Japanese and Germans have reduced costs and improved productivity while using American workers.

It wasn't for lack of trying to cooperate either. There was an effort to share management decisions with the union. The hope was that the real cost was not related to benefits and wages, but to motivational and environmental issues. Interestingly, this representative management was a throwback to republican workers systems of 1910s and 1920s. The idea then had been to hold off mandated unionization by the federal government. Companies such as Bethlehem Steel, Goodyear, and Firestone had been successful with this approach until New Deal politics labeled them as "company unions." The heavy industry unions of the 1930s would be independent of the company. The experience had left unions very distrustful of any effort to share management, fearing wages and rules might be discussed directly with the workers. It was this fear that was, at the same time in the 1980s, preventing the formation of employee improvement teams in the steel industry. Saturn at least tried to address the problem with a "new work system" approach.

Preceding the formation of Saturn, there was a "New Work" movement in the United States that hoped to form a partnership between labor and management. Saturn had hoped to improve on these new systems. A failing LTV Steel teamed up with Sumitomo Steel in 1990 to create a "New Work" system company to electro galvanize steel, known as LSE Electro Galvanizing. It was a new company with a 50–50 ownership agreement built literally in the shadow of LTV's giant — Cleveland Works. It had a special agreement with the United Steel Workers, much like Saturn's arrangement. The company allowed steelworkers to rotate jobs, where needed, and do maintenance and housekeeping work when the line shut down. Furthermore, it allowed for monthly maintenance to be contracted out. It was an amazing concession by the union. The wage and benefit issues remained similar, but pay was based on skill levels. Manning of the brand new plant was held to minimum levels. It had, in all ways, addressed the cost problems of the steel industry but only on a department level. The new company had fully addressed the wage and benefit cost disadvantage for galvanizing steel for the auto industry; the only problem was that the coating operation had to buy steel coils from LTV Steel with all the upstream wage costs built in.

The joint venture had been built by LTV to gain the Sumitomo superior coating technology and for Sumitomo to learn the American markets. The operation was manned by traditional LTV managers and Sumitomo engineers more interested in supplying Toyota's American operations than General Motors or Ford. The Japanese allowed poor quality to ship to General Motors while demanding perfection on Toyota's product. The Japanese were in a position to overrule American quality managers.[1] For those involved with the LSE joint venture, it became clear the "Japanese Revolution" was part myth and more the result of targeted levels of inspection. They seemed ignorant of the statistical techniques that were claimed to be at the root of their success. It left American middle managers disoriented after they had been trained in the superiority of Japanese statistical control, team management, and worker involvement. The secret was breaking out; the economic downturn in the 1990s would confirm the Japanese managers were mere mortals. Still, news people and politicians held to the myth that the Japanese were superior in operations, and the American decline was an American management issue. In particular, the Japanese quality approach would die a slow death in America.

Quality was never the real issue at these new work systems, however. It was the inability of the American managers to operate freely with the new work approach, and the Japanese managers' ability to manipulate the new work system. In the case of LSE and Saturn, the culture change in the workplace was too much, too fast. The union and the workers, for their part, compromised and adapted to the system. The American worker proved the most adaptable of all to the new work system. This worker acceptance was never achieved at Saturn. Still, the LSE operation that failed with LTV's second bankruptcy had achieved what Saturn had failed to do in addressing real costs at the plant level. But even at LSE, like Saturn, the company did not fully address all the product costs by failing to fully break with their parent companies. The Saturn's failure also had deep structural problems

The *Wall Street Journal* summarized the Saturn failure in 2009: "But make no mistake. The failure here isn't Mr. Penske [who pulled out of a last minute deal to buy Saturn]. Saturn was killed by its creators, GM and the UAW. The company starved Saturn for new products, and the union waged war against Saturn's labor reforms to keep them from spreading

---

1 Personal experience of author – who served as Manager of Quality Control at the company

to other GM factories."[1] By 2003, Saturn was no different than any poorly performing division of General Motors. Labor, pension, and benefit costs made it uncompetitive in the world market. The Obama Administration and bankers would shut the Saturn operation down in restructuring after the GM bankruptcy. Again, depending on which political party you belonged to, the fault was hung on either management or union.

The idea still exists that de-industrialization occurred because of lack of management and union cooperation, but experiments in employee participation and ownership have not proven out. Another Japanese "new work system" joint venture that was labeled a solution to America's uncompetitive manufacturing in the 1980s was New United Motors Manufacturing (NUMMI). While NUMMI would fail in 2010, it proved a brilliant marketing and business strategy for Toyota. In the end the workers, the union, and General Motors got little out of it.

NUMMI began with the flood of Japanese cars into California during the 1981–82 recession. The flood caused the shutdown of General Motors' Fremont, California, assembly plant in 1983. The shutdown threatened over 4,000 assembly and another 50,000 supplier jobs. Eventually in 1984, Toyota and General Motors formed NUMMI to keep the plant running. Toyota would have 70 percent ownership and control management. Toyota allowed the union to maintain generous wages and benefits, some of the best in the San Francisco area. Toyota had little interest in running a union assembly plant, but the political heat for protectionist legislation made it a strategic move to win public support. Toyota's contract only had one major demand — preventing transfers to other Toyota or General Motors plants. The Japanese at the time were looking to expand production in non-union states. NUMMI had been hailed at Saturn and LSE as the solution to global competition through cooperation. NUMMI, like Saturn and LSE Company, showed that employee participation on its own was not the solution to the problems raised by globalization.

The bottom line was that even with employee participation, Japanese style management, and Japanese technology, NUMMI was not competitive. The Japanese, however, had played American politics better than our good old boys. Over the next two decades, the Japanese expanded heavily into Southern non-union states, playing the political divide in America perfectly. The Japanese by 2004 were a major factor in American auto production. The Japanese transformed the original unity of American protectionism into a Democrat–Republican divide based on union

1 Paul Ingrassia, "Saturn Couldn't Escape GM's Dysfunctional Orbit," *Wall Street Journal,* October 2, 2009

and non-union voters and assuring the end of auto protectionism and nationalism. Maybe just as important to the Japanese leaving, the American public pointed fingers in different directions as to who was to blame. They had effectively eliminated the protectionist complains and reduced wages and benefits. In 2004, they were in a position to address their only union assembly plant of NUMMI. With General Motors, they pushed for reduction in wages and benefits at NUMMI. Then with the General Motors bankruptcy, General Motors pulled out and Toyota moved to close down its only union plant in 2010. The government rushed in with extended unemployment and other social services, playing the role of the concerned and sympatric government.

The union and the AFL-CIO mounted a boycott of Toyota along the old "buy American" type campaigns. It was a total failure, emblematic of the success of the Japanese strategy to divide and conquer. The South for decades had been the stronghold of "Buy American." Now tens of thousands of American jobs depended on Japanese automakers and their supply chain. In fairness, the Japanese have been part of a small re-industrialization movement. The idea of building plants and creating jobs in a foreign market is a positive approach to globalization. Of course, such re-industrialization in the US comes with much lower wages and benefits. Japan has the luxury of being a labor-short country which depends on foreign labor. The current phase of de-industrialization in America is fuelled by labor-rich countries such as China and India. China has a strategy of buying US government bonds, which doesn't help the American worker directly but creates an economic dependency at a higher level. China needs bonds or assets for trade with America — and by helping to keep the US dollar strong, they also create a favorable environment for Chinese imports into the United states

It may be closer to the truth that Saturn and the other new work systems such as NUMMI were over before they began. The fate of the American auto industry was set in April of 1947 at Lake Geneva, Switzerland. Under the banner of "free trade," American manufacturers were made uncompetitive with producers using subsistence-wage labor of the Third World. Instead of holding international capitalists and Third World countries to a higher standard of working conditions, free trade was more a political favor. Tariffs that might have been hinged on the level of wages and benefits of these oppressed workers were promoted as anti-capitalistic and even unfair to the Third World. Allowing subsistence workers to compete with American labor was posited as a way to distribute wealth to the needy countries, when in fact the workers of these countries were subjected to even worse conditions. Without addressing this, we will see more Saturns.

The efforts of many new American work systems showed that the problem was not poor labor relations, per se. Yet the myth continues today that competitiveness is based in labor and labor relations. Politicians and the banks have once again drawn our focus elsewhere. The problem is an economic one, and the only solution will be one that addresses that.

Free trade should be based on the equality of workers and working conditions. Tariffs would allow America to use its economic power to be the city on the hill, a shining example spreading an ideal of worker treatment and higher living standards for the majority of the population. Furthermore, our current government and economic strategy forces pension and health costs into the products we produce, while allowing unprivileged workers elsewhere to ship their product in without any such burden. Conservatives who have in the past supported tariffs to cover such workers differences are told that you cannot have capitalism without free trade; this is accepted as dogma. Liberals pressure companies such as Wal-Mart to take on nations such as China to eliminate worker abuse. The status quo since the 1960s has been the de-industrialization of America. The public is totally misled as they see the cheap goods but see their paychecks disappear at the same time, and neither party tries to attack the status quo.

Chapter 16. Tale of the Last Two Cities

The loss of industry in America has been devastating. It has brought ruin to cities large and small, and to whole regions, from the East Coast to the West Coast, and especially the Great Lakes area. Some towns fell precipitously while others faded away slowly, with moments of hope, like Youngstown. Like the fall of Rome, it is hard to pinpoint the precise date for the fall of American heavy industry. Some historians of the future may place that date as 2009 with the bankruptcy of General Motors. For the workers of America, that was more than a stock market event. Workers might look to the final collapse of Weirton, West Virginia, as the end of American steel and the collapse of Flint, Michigan, for the auto industry. These were the last outposts of America's industrial empire. These were one-industry towns, like Youngstown of two decades earlier. They were the home of America's great upper middle class workers of an earlier time. The plants were a "family" business for the workers. At their peak, Flint and Weirton had two of the highest per capita income in the United States. They were cities where family, community, and work were synonymous. They hung on into the new century with little but a fading hope of a return to past glories.

The final devastation of the American auto industry came in the new century; Detroit's sundog outpost cities such as Flint would fall in the 1990s. Flint closed its last auto assembly plant in 1999 and that signaled the end of American dominance in auto production.

Flint began and ended with Buick. Flint had been a major auto producer even prior to Henry Ford's Detroit operation. In 1904, William Durant formed Buick Motors; and by 1908, Buick was the largest manufacturer of automobiles. In the 1920s, William Durant formed General Motors in Flint. While Detroit often claims to be the birthplace of the automotive industry, Flint was an irrefutable claim to the birthplace of the United Auto Workers Union in 1937. In that year, Flint, even more than Detroit, was a true auto town with 50,000 of its 150,000 inhabitants working in auto plants. In the 1970s, General Motors employed 80,000 workers in Flint. Flint achieved the top income per capita in the nation in those years. Today over 30 percent of the city lives below the poverty line.

The death blow came to Flint was the closing of the Buick assembly plant. Flint had been headquarters for General Motors Buick Division, and the city had the largest GM manufacturing complex in the world. General Motors had not let its massive Buick assembly plant become obsolete, and the company worked hard to keep GM in town. In the early 1980s, the plant was completely retooled and robots were added. The famous Buick supplier city was built to assure Just-In-Time supply. Amazingly, despite all those efforts, by 1999 the plant was closed and a few years later demolished.

That same year General Motors spun off its Flint Delphi spark plug plant, but it continued operating. Flint hung on with its engine plant and auto parts factories, but barely. Like Youngstown of the 1980s, there were moments of hope that GM factories would be purchased by other corporations. Flint's auto employment fell from 80,000 at its peak to 8,000 in 2010. Delphi spark plug was, however, non-competitive by the 2000s with wages of $27 an hour versus domestic non-union plants at $12 an hour. Non-union American labor, however, was the least of the problem. General Motors was paying $1.70 for spark plugs from Flint, when they could have bought them from China and India for $1.05. Worse yet, those $1.70 spark plugs were actually costing $2.05 to make.[1] The unemployment numbers in the 2000s were spun to make the problem appear less severe; most of those who lost their jobs were no longer counted as "unemployed" because they had quit looking for work, moved out of town, or were transferred to welfare rolls.

Flint experienced a slow, painful decline. Its population reached 200,000 in the 1960s; today it is 100,000. The city struggled from the

---

1 "The Fall of Flint." *The Detroit News*, December 11, 2005

beginning of the 21st century with financial problems. Crime reached levels only exceeded by Detroit. In 2011, the state had to appoint a financial emergency manager to run the bankrupt city. Many of Flint's tallest buildings were unoccupied and surrounded by warning signs for falling debris. Gangs outnumbered police. Thousands of homes were demolished. Crime and lack of city services made the city uninhabitable — except for those with no way out. Those who could moved out in the 1990s.

Most Americans would be shocked to see how their fellow citizens are living in Flint and Detroit. No trade war that free trade economists warned of could have produced such devastation. Politicians like to ignore these economic waste lands, focusing on some vision of a bright future in the America of the post-industrial era. Political efforts brought back a few automotive operations, but the local workforce is not prepared to handle the newer technical operations. There are few high school graduates among the population under 35 years old. Flint is far past the tipping point where new industries can bring a solution. Union labor, crime, and deteriorating infrastructure make it an unlikely choice for large manufacturing to move in.

Critics were quick to point out the rise of the massive Toyota assembly plant in Georgetown, Kentucky, during the decline of Flint. Both General Motors management and the United Auto Workers shared the blame, according to the press. But neither set of these critics really understood the problem. Yes, the Georgetown Toyota auto workers were paid less than half the wages and benefits of the General Motors Flint worker. Yes, Toyota had better quality. But even these disadvantages were minor compared to the invisible elephant in the room. General Motors had huge legacy costs in pensions and health care benefits that Toyota had avoided accruing. General Motors had made those commitments to the union over the years, under government pressure. The government had proudly taken credit for unionization and high wages in the auto industry but accepts no blame for its decline.

Now, the government criticized a bloated industry unable to compete with other countries. Liberal politicians blamed management for lack of investment and innovation. Conservative politicians blamed overpaid workers. Economic consultants advised that America would "have to adjust" to a new competitive world. They seemed to forget the government role in bloating the industry; and the economic consultants that had forced up wages and benefits in the 1930s, 1940s, and 1950s. Not that the government was wrong in helping workers get better wages in the glory years of auto profits. Where the government failed was in refusing to protect the auto industry during the transition to the new global market, which the American government had created. Americans were clearly being punished for their success in an effort to bring higher incomes and the accompanying blind faith in capitalism to the rest of the world, too.

While convincing the rest of the world that our system is the best system is not a morally bad mission, it should not have been done at the expense of American workers. The company and the workers were owed that protection in tariffs and investment; or in today's language, it was their right. The government decided it could do better by training unemployed auto workers and beefing up safety-net benefits for those who were to lose their jobs, in place of maintaining the auto industry.

When it all failed, the politicians made the city a ward of the state. The government strategy has not helped Flint or its citizens. In fact, considering the economic costs of totally free trade, the strategy of de-industrializing America seems like treason. A large part of America's debt has to do with families, towns and cities struggling to maintain a pale semblance of the good life they once knew, despite the damage of this de-industrialization strategy.

Weirton, West Virginia, like Flint, was a city built around its industry. In this case, it was the steel industry. Pittsburgh steelmaker Ernst Weir built his company under the protection provided by the McKinley tariff system in the early 1900s. Industrialist Weir moved his steel company to the village of Holidays Cove on the West Virginia side of the Ohio River in 1909. Weir built what would become a fully integrated steel mill for the manufacture of tin plate. By the 1950s, Weirton Steel was West Virginia's largest employer and the world's largest tin plate manufacturer in the world. The city of Weirton was a real steel town, totally dependent on Weirton Steel. Weirton Steel in the 1920s built the city's streets and sewers. It formed a municipal improvement organization to manage all the city services.

In 1929, Weirton Steel merged with Detroit's Michigan Steel and M.A. Hanna Corporation to form National Steel, the world's largest supplier of tin plate and galvanized steel. Weirton had prospered under the paternal guidance of Ernst Weir. Much like Essen and Krupp Steel in Germany, it was a self-contained kingdom of steel. A community of Weirton Steel families worked and lived there. The hills above the city were blackened with iron dust and sulfurous fumes. Still, it was a proud and happy place to work and live. Injured steelworkers were given a life time of reduced labor work in order to maintain their families. Sons were assured a high-paying job in the mill. The workers were the best paid in the steel business. Weirton had its own union, which averaged $4 an hour more than the industry overall, which kept the Weirton workers from joining the United Steelworkers (who were paid less).

Life was good; and for all the talk of pollution, there was lots of hunting, fishing and trapping nearby. Many workers made extra money searching the hills for native ginseng to sell. For the younger workers, Steubenville, Ohio, was just across the Ohio River, offering Vegas type entertainment. Families would drive their kids at Christmastime to nearby Pittsburgh to visit the department stores' toy lands. There was a fair amount of non-violent crime, mostly related to the gambling which was a beloved past time of Weirton Steel workers. A bet could be placed at any time on anything in the steel mill. The "Tin Can Festival" every year offered free meals from tin can products. Families could afford to take real vacations. The town gambled but also had a big heart, giving much of its income to local churches and charities. It was the major source of income tax for the state. It was a true middle class working town and iconic of the prosperity of the 1950s. Today, those who remember, remember it as Camelot.

Weirton started to feel the pains of competition with the new steel mills of Europe and Japan in the 1960s. While short of capital, the company did modernize with the Basic Oxygen Process and new steelmaking operations. The recession of 1972 combined with foreign steel was too much. Weirton had to deeply cut employment, something it had always tried to avoid. It was a serious blow to morale. Weirton and National Steel would continue its decline until 1982. That year, National Steel put the Weirton operation up for sale.

Then Weirton put together an employee buyout. In 1984 the employees formed the largest ESOP in the United States. The workers gave back 32 percent of their wages in the package. All pensions prior to 1982 would revert to National Steel, which would give the company the competitive edge it needed. Lower wages, legacy costs, and benefits were all addressed. A new cooperative labor approach was enacted. It was a good deal for all. It addressed all that the free trade economists had assured us was the "real" problems. National Steel had estimated it would cost twice as much to shut the plant down. The company would once again find profitability, and optimism returned to the town.

Weirton was once again an employee-focused company with employee participation teams. America's big steel companies looked in awe at the Weirton turnaround. By 1984, Weirton was earning $41 a ton more on steel than any other U.S. steel company. It was estimated that Weirton had a $3 to $4 a ton labor cost advantage, a $3 a ton quality advantage, and a $4 productivity advantage. Weirton and its employees had done everything that anyone could have asked for, and still had reasonable benefits and wages in the United States. Weirton was being hailed as a new model to bring the steel industry to profitability. ESOP workers proved extremely flexible, even cutting jobs to help put together capital to modernize. Unfortunately, Weirton's success came at the expense of the other steel companies. Weirton took market share from other domestic steel companies, but foreign steel still had a wage and a health care advantage.

By the end of the 1980s, foreign steel had targeted tin plate and galvanized markets for more penetration. In Congress, Weirton's success became an excuse to limit tariff protection. Economists could point to Weirton as being able to compete with imports. Still, the real issue had been, and still was, free trade policies. The new wave of steel imports of the 1990s was even cheaper. No one could expect Weirton employees to drop down to Chinese wages and benefits.

Without protection in the 1990s, foreign steelmakers took more market share. Weirton was crippled and unable to raise capital. To fund improvements, Weirton took the company public — against the wishes of many ESOP members. Public ownership did not fit well into the cooperative spirit that had been achieved at Weirton. Labor relations returned to the low of former years. In any case, the public stock offering didn't raise the capital needed. Without protection from the government to allow it some precious time, Weirton began to lose money as foreign steel undercut prices. Weirton was no longer the darling of Washington but just another company that couldn't compete in a global economy. By 2003, Weirton Steel, the state's fifth largest employer, went into bankruptcy.

International Steel Group purchased Weirton Steel in 2004 and then sold it to the India-based multinational steel maker Mittal Steel (ArcelorMittal) a year later. ISG had promised a rosy picture of bringing on line a second blast furnace. To facilitate the deal, Weirton's Independent Steelworkers Union cut jobs from 3,000 to 2,000 and eliminated costly work rules. Mittal offered a less rosy picture, idling the hot end of the operation. The Weirton union once again offered more cuts and savings, but Mittal showed little interest. Mittal had purchased the once great American steelmaking operations at Burns Harbor, Indiana Harbor, and

Sparrows Point. Weirton was the swing plant. These other plants were United Steelworkers Union. Mittal had made a secret agreement with the USW union in exchange for support of the merger, saying that non-USW workers would be laid off first in any downsizing.[1] Sadly, unions had found it necessary to adopt the same "survival of the fitness" strategies as the owners.

As usual, Washington huffed, puffed, and decried the Mittal takeover. Weirton, West Virginia, was represented by two of the nation's most powerful Democrats in Jay Rockefeller and Robert Byrd; yet in real terms, nothing was done to help the workers except the usual extension of benefits and training for those who were "displaced." The worker buyouts included cash payments of $60,000 down to $35,000 plus extended health care benefits. Federal money went to "help" workers make the transition at the Rockefeller Career Center. The workers once again lost, with no political help in saving the plant. Republican candidates had been defeated with union money and so had no interest in helping, while Democrats were moving on to government unions where the votes and money were. Of course, there were the usual sympathetic press statements by politicians. State and local government started to invest in campaigns to replace the industry that they had just lost. The political backlash that normally would follow such a disaster was, as in the past, diffused by the exodus of unemployed workers to other states.

The once massive integrated steelmaking at Weirton was being closed, piece by piece. Mittal had little interest in the hot end of Weirton Steel. The coating lines and Weirton product market made ArcelorMittal the world's largest tinplate producer. Employment continued to decline at Weirton, reaching a mere 1,000 employees in 2010. The once major employer was ranked 67th in the state in 2010. Ironically, a new Wal-Mart in Weirton was built, and the store is now the state's largest employer. Politicians had turned Wal-Mart into a sort of straw man for the decline of union jobs, when in fact Wal-Mart is merely a symptom of a failed national manufacturing policy. What is left of the city struggles on. It looks to the usual solutions to de-industrialization of building casinos and Wal-Marts.

The devastation of our historic cities is unbelievable to those who have not experienced it firsthand. The average American who thinks open air gunfire throughout the night is something from Hollywood has never stayed in a rust belt city. War protestors fight to spare American

---

1 *Form 20-F, 2005 Mittal Steel*, submitted to U.S. Securities and Exchange Commission, p. 105

lives on foreign battlefields but ignore the much greater loss of life in our cities every day. Senators take to the floor to decry the loss of American soldiers, ignoring the overwhelming death rate on our city streets. It is hard to imagine that an armed invasion of America would have caused such devastation compared to de-industrialization. Our cities probably would have recovered faster from the 1950 nuclear strike we so feared. The alleged trade wars of the 1930s were far less damaging to our cities. The huge continuing economic and social costs of our 60 years of Mont Pèlerin economic policy are staggering. Whatever was the goal, what we ended up with is open gang warfare in our cities.

The loss of manufacturing has reduced our tax base while requiring increased welfare spending, and this means there is less money for our schools and social services. We argue over whether taxes or spending is the solution to debt without looking at our policies that kill industry, the engine of growth. Our government, lacking income to fully sustain itself, is starting to fail. Yet Americans are still being told (and seem to accept) that the solution is in more of the same. Maybe it is time for a new group of outcast economists to meet at Weirton Heights and discuss America's policies for an industrial future and scientific tariff management.

CHAPTER 17. A POST INDUSTRIAL AGE?

"The King has no clothes."

For many, the question is, who's to blame? Clearly there are lots of participants to choose from. The campaign to destroy US manufacturing has deeper roots than management, unions, government, banks, environmentalists, economists, Japanese, the Chinese, and others. Somewhere, this nation decided we no longer needed to be the manufacturing world leader. We saw it at a Lordstown, which would become a turning point. Without a national vision, the nation's manufacturing was buffeted by problem after problem. Lack of cooperation through a national policy left various interest groups to fight and destroy manufacturing. Cooperation, coordination, and compromise were missing. We abdicated our right to set our own trade policies to international bodies such as the WTO. The lack of a national vision for manufacturing tells us why US industry went down and at the same time explains why China is so successful. The secret is not, in fact, China's cheap labor, lack of unions, lack of regulation, and disregard for environmental concerns. It is that China wants to be an industrial power, and its policy reflect that. It is determination, and yes, even nationalism, that drives manufacturing. It is the shared determination to meet a national goal that helped China achieve its cost advantage and worker productivity coupled with light regulation. They had taken the national spirit and goal setting of a centrally-planned government and applied it to a capitalistic economic model. This is the unmistakable lesson of history. It was the secret behind the "Japanese

Revolution" of the 1970s and the golden manufacturing years of America in the 1890s through 1920s.

Another current contributing to the tidal wave of de-industrialization was the polarization of the nation on basic beliefs. Hayek's free-trade economic positions were widely accepted because nuance was lost and the debate was simplified to black-or-white views and lack of compromise. You were either a Keynesian or Hayekian as far as American economists were concerned. There would be no middle road. Flag waving, nationalistic conservatives adopted "free trade" because they espoused the complete Hayekian philosophy, especially avoiding government intervention; they feared that Hayek's 'no government' approach had to be accepted as a package, that tinkering around the margins could weaken the overall argument for lower taxes and less government spending. Liberals came on board because the Hayekian view offered a distribution of wealth and international governance in the philosophy. Unions understood the deeper problem, but they were already tied to one party. At best, the unions were placated by short term highly focused tariffs over the years, or various plant closing benefits. At worst, they were given endless years of retraining and better unemployment benefits. Both liberals and conservatives dug in their heels, preventing the two political parties from even debating free trade. Interestingly, theoretical polarization on economics produced one of the few things both parties seemed to agree on, but for different reasons! It also followed the capitalism that fueled America for almost 150 years was not really a true belief of Adam Smith. Capitalism in the new order could only exist on an international level.

Economists assured politicians we would turn a corner. Creative destruction would transform industrial America. We just needed to stay on the painful course. The growing structural unemployment, rising numbers of welfare recipients, poor, or those in poverty, if you prefer, could be explained by other factors depending on which political side you were on. Reasons varied from laziness, lack of taxes, too many taxes, too little or too much regulation, unions, corporate greed, and so forth. But rarely was it mentioned that there appeared to be a programmatic lack of support for industry, for manufacturing, which had employed tens of millions, created wealth and mobility, and elevated cities beyond the poverty of the present. There was, of course, the mythical promise of a high tech information economy that would follow de-industrialization. Americans were told this post-industrial age would provide high paying jobs for our highly educated population.

We seem stuck in a polarized nation, unable to come together to address tough questions, since industry was been dramatically reduced. Was Detroit better off with the highly paid but worn-out workers who could send the next generation to college, or now with its 40 percent unemployment and 60 percent literacy rate? Do the smoke-free skies of Youngstown and Akron make life more enjoyable for the hopelessly unemployed? Have our schools improved by losing tax income from industry? Has international trade made goods so cheap that we can afford a better lifestyle even if we are out of work? Are the cleaner rivers a source of food for the masses that line up in cities every day for a meal? Have our roads improved now that we have fewer heavy trucks? Does the sound of bullets make for a better urban rest than the hammer forges of the old factories? Do you know anyone who has launched a new career by accepting re-training for the old factory job? Where would you rather spend a night — in the open in an underdeveloped country or in downtown Detroit? What happened to our highly educated engineers, scientists, and post graduates who were to lead us in this new post-industrial era? How is the nation to employ the ever increasing number of young people lacking a high school diploma in a post-industrial era?

The economists of the Austrian and Chicago schools and followers of the brain trust of the Mont Pèlerin Society need to be asked some questions as well. Whose interests are being served? For at least 60 years, the very mention of protecting an American industry generated cries of trade wars. Nations like China feel free to use trade as a form of economic warfare; even the American military is coming to believe economics may well be a more effective weapon than traditional arms. For workers, there are more questions. Should a government that was so ready to ask its workers to fight political wars have ignored the willingness of American workers to fight a trade war? Has the huge economic sacrifice of American industries actually created a more peaceful world? Would a trade war have been more destructive than the last 60 years of de-industrialization? Where are the massive increases in exports that were to offset losses in imports? It may be time to ask if these elite theorists actually wear clothes.

Another question that might be asked — has a bit of global wealth redistribution been worth the 60 years of massive costs of unemployment benefits, welfare costs and related programs, urban re-development funding, loss of taxes, endless decades of re-training, social programs for readjustment, and food stamp programs? The loss of taxes has been talked about part as of our national debt. Would we not have been much better off by simply protecting our key industries at least at the level of our own needs? The price to workers individually has also been devastating. Even the blessed who have avoided job loss are working for less pay and benefits. Many Americans might willingly trade their inner city homes for the relative safety of many in the so-called poor nations.

Of course, there are the few who will argue that the nation has moved beyond manufacturing; we no longer need to make things, but we can make our way in the world by the value of our thinking about things. It certainly reflects the popular view in academia that we are moving beyond our industrial heritage to a better world. Others see de-industrialization as necessary distribution of wealth on an international level. The post-industrial world is being unified as the old nationalism of the past is relaxed. No matter what one's perspective, today's manufacturing scene resembles the vision of the Mont Pèlerin in 1947.

We are told that this is the "Information Age" and that is where America should be focused. For decades, many white collar workers such as accountants and engineers thought they were beyond the job losses of globalization. Or at least, surely the retailing jobs of this new age would be secure. Only now we see a rapid shift to online sales. Retail is eliminating jobs and only some new openings occur for software engineers. Electronic technology has globalized the world of information and data. Indian workers are even being used in McDonald's drive thru. This is the "post-industrial" world; it means that even information jobs can be lost to cheaper labor. There are few jobs that cannot be outsourced. Doctors can even perform operations using robots thousands of miles away.

What does post-industrial really mean, and how does the American dream play out in such an environment? It was popular in the 1980s to look at the move from industrial to post-industrial as a "paradigm shift," some inevitable and neutral change. For the last twenty years, universities have been offering courses on "post-industrial" everything in the Liberal Arts, Business, and even the Engineering colleges. The general idea is that post-industrialism is the natural evolution of society to a higher plane. Some even call it creative destruction. Post-industrialism is heralded as the Information Age. Mental work is supposed to replace menial physical work. Other nations will do the dirty work of making things, while America will remain the great financial and innovation center, a green society built on well-paid, educated knowledge workers. And we, the people, will finally have the time and means to address our highest needs such as self-actualization. That was the blueprint for the updated American dream.

In reality, the new edifice is falling flat. The literacy rate in our cities is at Stone Age levels, despite pouring more and more tax-payers' dollars into remedial efforts to cover education costs when manufacturing corporations leave town. High school graduation rates of over 60 percent in our cities are called "miraculous." The literacy rate in cities like Detroit is lower than in the Third World. Our math skills are rated below 40th along the world's nations. All of this while being told that post-industrial Americans are too well-educated for the old factory jobs of the past. Where, then, should those who could not complete high school seek to work? America's inventive geniuses still bring in revolutionary technology such as the PC computer, only to find they have to send production overseas as an employment gift to other countries because they cannot find competitive manufacturing conditions and tech skills among their fellow Americans. Today, we lack the engineers needed for the next advance in computers.

In a post-industrial era American greatness is an impossibility, and the reasons for that go far beyond literacy rate alone. With the decline in industry, the graduation of American engineers and scientists has also been in spiraling decline. In many of our most prestigious colleges, if you took away the international students, the science and engineering classrooms would be empty. Apple and Microsoft — and others requiring far less exotic technical expertise, say that their operations are locating overseas because they can hire engineers at every level of production.

Our rust belt is the new Third World, except that many Third World countries are better in math and science. Colleges offer courses in conflict resolution, game playing, and relaxation rather than science and engineering. Popular culture hardly glorifies mathematicians and engineers. Teachers are not the respected figures they once were. How would it occur to young people that making a hard mental effort is the road to respect? The nation has a record number of families on the welfare rolls, some of them for generations. Government representatives talk as if unemployment checks and food stamps, paid for by those who are still working, were an economic stimulus.

Free-market capitalism as currently practiced in the US is no longer viewed as the ideal. Our original approach, a kind of national capitalism, produced results that were good for Americans; today's international capitalism is good for transnational corporations. This kind of capitalism is hated more than communism and even National Socialism. In fact, surveys show American youth cannot define the difference between capitalism and socialism. America now looks to Europe as the city on the hill: their various models mix capitalism with a large measure of social protection. Old-style American nationalism and patriotism are now considered arrogant. The public perception is moving toward a more moderate stance, one of normal national pride combined with a desire to protect American jobs. The word "exceptionalism" (in the sense that America, right or wrong, was somehow inherently superior to all other nations) is not even in Microsoft's speller checker and most dictionaries. Americans are coming to view themselves as just another country of the world, of no particular significance, that uses more than its fair share of resources. The Mont Pèlerin economists have generated a new concept for American acceptance: "shrinking to greatness."[1] Free trade economics has moved from the means for growth to creative destruction to "shrinking to greatness" in 60 years, with little hard questioning at the highest levels of government and academia.

Thus it is time to suggest that that the king has no clothes. In the once-great cities of America, you can see all of the king's tattoos. There has been little to celebrate other than the opening of a new Pro Bass (selling goods made in China) and the regional gambling casino. Retraining, which had become a growth industry in itself, was supposed to be a means, not an end. But the college degree no longer leads to a secure career or even a job. Serious educators see little financial value in going to college. Most Americans today will not do better than their parents. The once feared military industrial complex is dependent on foreign parts to function. Even the last truly big growth industry — government — has reached its limit as the taxpayers cannot cover the costs. Only the health care industry growth remains a "bright" spot as the population ages, depression rises, and personal health declines.

More of the same free trade will not get us on a new path. The latest idea is that we can be the international banking center for the world. Banking today is driven by the big banks. The local and regional banks, which were built on industry and industrial workers, are minor players. The big banks are, by nature, multinational and international, with little dedication to any one nation. Smaller banks fail as we support those "too big to fail." They have proved successful in creatively bundling our bad debt and exporting it.

Probably the one group (after the economists who provide the theoretical justifications) that bears the most responsibility and yet receive

---

1 Edward Glaiser, *The Triumph of the City*, (New York: Penguin Press, 2011), p. 64

the least blame is the big banks. The industrial builders of the nation such as Henry Ford, Andrew Carnegie, and Harvey Firestone had always seen big banks as a potential danger to the survivability of American industry. They believed in regional and local banks that were more responsive to emerging industries. Even early on, New York bankers such as the House of Morgan supported international trade versus industry. Men like George Westinghouse and Henry Ford would not deal with the big New York banks because they lacked a local orientation. While American banks have prospered much from de-industrialization, they are seeing the new industrial powers create their own mega-banks. In the end, even the co-architects of de-industrialization, American bankers, are seeing the writing on the wall.

The solution would represent another book, but I'd like to end where I started — with some 1820 observations on American industry: "In passing along the highway one frequently sees large and spacious buildings, with the glass broken out the windows, the shutters hanging in ruinous disorder, without any appearance of activity and enveloped in solitary gloom." Henry Clay would work another 30 years and form the major political party of the Whigs to restore American industry. The Whigs would give birth to a new generation of Republican protectionists such as Abraham Lincoln, James Garfield, and William McKinley, who, in 1890, made America an industrial power and from there, a global military and political power. The national economic focus of the Whigs and morphed Republicans gave America a way to vote for American industrial growth. Later in the 1930s, the Democrats took over the torch of protectionism. By 1990, both parties looked away from protectionism, losing track of the fundamental basis of national strength.

The start of a solution is simple. Americans still want to be a nation that makes things. To get back on that track will require an industrial vision for the nation — that of Alexander Hamilton. Hamilton's two-page policy statement in 1794 turned the nation's mission from that of agricultural to industrial. This simple manufacturing policy set the infrastructure for decades of details. It was similar to that of China, which set a national manufacturing policy in the 1980s. For China, that manufacturing mission was independent of its communist social structure. The fact is China's success is the result of a national decision, not its resources or cheap labor. America's decline has likewise been a decision not the result of unions, poor management, imports, or expensive labor. It took Henry Clay's vision and 70 years of political action and leadership to fulfill; but those windows were replaced in 1880, ushering in a golden age of manufacturing. Maybe someday the Whigs of Henry Clay will rise again to repair our economic windows.

Others see the seeds of re-birth in innovation coming from the libraries and cultural institutes of the very cities built by the paternal capitalists. One historian sees the cities that fared best under de-industrialization as those having the best educational resources.[1] It is in Boston, with its educational core, that we see resilience. In Pittsburgh, robots are tested on old steel slag dumps by researchers at Carnegie-Mellon University. Both cities have extensive libraries, art museums, universities, and science centers. The Smithsonian also believes that science and history museums can act as fuel for innovation. But even having the resources (and America has both energy and innovation) means little without the political will.

---

1 Edward Glaiser, *The Triumph of the City*, (New York: Penguin Press, 2011), pp. 45

Chapter 18. Maybe We Need to Revisit a Whig Party Platform?

For a manufacturer, it is a simple problem of exports and imports. Of course, stating such a simplistic proposal puts your credibility on the line. Political polarization takes away the power of workers to fight for American jobs. Since the demise of the Whigs in 1858 no party has held all the tools for such a fight.

Workers today are divided first by the question of union and non-union. Then they are divided by an endless number of emotionally hot social issues that the press works to keep alive and burning. The American consumer is the American worker, and so he is torn between the desire for cheap prices versus the need for a job. Furthermore, economists tell us all, as politicians, voters, workers, and as consumers, that the problem with American industry is high wages, poor management, and a lack of innovation. People are led to fight over details rather than to analyze the big picture. This polarization allows only for black and white decisions. Industry is seen as a source of pollution, while it is forgotten that industry is the wealth generator that has funded our best museums, colleges, and cultural institutions. Politicians attack companies (gaining consumer sympathy) for moving overseas. The companies are even pictured as unpatriotic by a government that offers them no help or even an industrial policy. Since the days of Alexander Hamilton and Henry Clay, the nation has lacked a national manufacturing policy.

China has a national goal to become the world's manufacturer. Its dedication to that goal goes beyond politics. They are willing to set aside their other divisive issues and band together on this. The struggle over communist and capitalist theory is always second to goal of economic development. The building of a factory is paramount over political philosophy. National strength trumps local or factional politics. (Economists argue whether they are communists or capitalists. What they are is Whigs.)

No economist could expect to make a career advocating a return to Whig party policies, but for manufacturers such a development is needed. Furthermore, no self-respecting Democrat or Republican would be comfortable as a Whig. The Whigs valued the output of a nation, not the value of its dollar. For a Whig, exports measure greatness, not imports. Whigs saw government as a tool to create manufacturing and economic prosperity. Whigs opposed unionization while demanding government projects to create jobs. Whigs believed in protecting American industry through tariffs and didn't mind government overspending — if it expanded industry. Whigs believed the role of the Federal Reserve was to pump money into industry and job expansion. Whigs had little time for social issues. They tended to be hawks or isolationists, based on what was better at the time for the home front. While they were nationalists, they accepted immigrants as a source of labor. They cared little for international politics. The Whigs would be (and were) at home in the Rust Belt.

The Whigs' main argument is that the greatest nations have always been manufacturers and exporters. To a degree, the Whig argument of how America should attain economic greatness goes to Alexander Hamilton's first report on manufacturing in 1792, Henry Clay's Whig Party platform in 1823, Abraham Lincoln's protectionist's policy, and lastly, William McKinley's manufacturing miracle of the 1890s. All of these approaches to the economy were practical approaches based on prosperity, not economic theory. The approach was to focus on the needs of the nation, not the world.

The "Report on Manufacturers" (also called the Treatise on Manufacturing) is considered the magnum opus of Alexander Hamilton, first Secretary of the Treasury. It was presented to Congress on December 5, 1791, and is considered the guiding document for the economic principles of the United States. The "Report on Manufactures" was followed by specific reports on banking and credit. It was analogous to an economic Declaration of Independence to be followed by constitutional specifics.

It was originally opposed by then Secretary of State, Thomas Jefferson. The disagreement between Hamilton and Jefferson was derived from two different visions. Jefferson saw the United States as an agrarian nation where manufacture would be done on large plantations. Hamilton foresaw an urban nation built on manufacturing cities. By Jefferson's death in 1825, he came to accept Hamilton's vision of an industrial America. Still, the political parties were focused on constitutional issues.

The Report on Manufacturers was considered a blend of Mercantilism as practiced in England and the practices of Jean-Baptiste Colbert of France. It would reject the more recent ideas of Adam Smith's free trade and minimal government interference. It would be the economic foundation of the emerging Federalist Party. The Federalist Party believed in positive government input into economic development. Hamilton understands that workers and owners are needed for economic development.

Ultimately, Hamilton's ideas would be incorporated in the "American System" of Henry Clay's Whig Party in the 1830s. The young Whig, Abraham Lincoln, would incorporate it into the newly formed Republican Party. Later in the 1880s, William McKinley would make it the cornerstone of Republican Party platforms for decades to come. Much of Alexander Hamilton's vision of the United States has come to pass. How did he arrive at his views?

In 1790, Hamilton faced a financial mess. The country lacked international and domestic credit. The currency was worthless, and soldiers paid in script were near rebellion. While free, the country was facing financial collapse. Alexander Hamilton believed that America would fail if it did not excel in manufacturing. He reasoned this from his experience as a young military officer under George Washington in the Revolutionary War. The army had suffered from lack of arms, gunpowder, uniforms, iron implements, and ammunition, which nearly cost America the war. American manufacturing lacked capacity, and the success of the British blockage nearly crushed the struggling Centennial Army. In the report, Hamilton noted, "The extreme embarrassment of the United States during the late war, from incapacity of supplying themselves, are still matter of keen recollection." After that experience, Hamilton believed that the United States needed to build a strong manufacturing sector if it wanted to remain free.

Furthermore, the country lacked a transportation system to supply the army. Alexander Hamilton stated: "Those hands, which may be deprived of business by the cessation of commerce, may be occupied in various kinds of manufactures and other internal improvements. If . . .

manufactures should . . . take root among us, they will pave the way, still more, to the future grandeur and the glory of America." Hamilton argued that national industries should be supported through protective tariffs, direct subsidies, a national banking system, and a national transportation system. Hamilton refuted Adam Smith's work on the basis that it was based on agricultural society.

The following is an important excerpt from the Report on Manufacturing: "But though it were true, that the immediate and certain effect of regulations controlling the competition of foreign with domestic fabrics was an increase of price, it is universally true, that the contrary is the ultimate effect with every successful manufacture. When a domestic manufacture has attained to perfection, and has engaged in the prosecution of it a competent attend the importation of foreign commodities, it can be afforded, and accordingly seldom or never fails to be sold cheaper, in process of time, than was the foreign article for which it is a substitute. The internal competition, which takes place, soon does away everything like monopoly, and by degrees reduces the price of the article to the minimum of a reasonable profit on the capital employed. These accords with reason of the thing, and with experience. Whence it follows, that it is in the interest of a community, with a view to eventual and permanent economy, to encourage the growth of manufactures, in a national view, a temporary enhancement of price must always be well compensated by a permanent reduction of it."

Hamilton argued for tariffs not only to protect infant industries but also be a source of revenue for the government. A Congress in need of money to pay off war debt quickly adopted this part of the Report. Most opponents saw the Whig Party as a political party dedicated to the economic development of the United States through modernization, infrastructure, manufacturing self-sufficiency, and protectionism. Initially, the Whig Party was an economic movement free of any social issues. Its platform was designed by Kentucky congressman, Henry Clay, and was known as the "American System" in the 1820s. The Whigs had seen decades of de-industrialization.

The Whig Party would have four presidents — William Harrison (1841), John Tyler (1841–1845), Zachary Taylor (1849–1850), and Millard Fillmore (1850–1853). Abraham Lincoln was a Whig turned republican after the demise of the Whig Party. The Whig Party roots went back to Alexander Hamilton's "Treatise on Manufacturing" in 1794, believing in the need for manufacturing to be at the center of national economic policy. The Whig Party took in old Federalists who believed in federal funds for infrastructure such as canal and roads. The difference is the Whigs saw tariffs as the way to finance such internal improvements. They argued that tariffs would not bring the resistance and outcry of taxes as seen in the Whiskey Rebellion. Of course, many farmers and Southerners argued that tariffs were a "tax" on basic goods via a price increase of imported goods such as woolens, iron products, glass, and clothes. The Whigs countered that the use of domestic production would boost the overall economy. Henry Clay was the founder and guiding light of the Whig Party. The basis of the Whig Party would be the economic system of Henry Clay known as the "American System." Some historians have called it "economic nationalism." Clay was able to tie economic nationalism to Manifest Destiny.

Henry Clay had been a supporter and follower of Alexander Hamilton. In his junior years in the Senate, he advocated a strong national bank and a national road system. Often Clay favored the good of the nation over his own constituents in Kentucky. His oratory, compromising skills, and patriotism brought him quickly to the position of Speaker of the House. Clay not only fashioned the position of House Speaker, but he formed the powerful Ways and Means Committee with another future president, James Garfield, which would be the pedestal to launch the career of William McKinley years later, and lead to the Republican Party's reign of protectionism from 1860 to 1920. Clay also created a Committee on Manufactures to help stimulate American manufacturing as Alexander Hamilton had suggested years earlier. Clay centralized legislative power under the position of Speaker. Clay used the power to create a national infrastructure for early industrial America. His vision of an industrial empire took him from Jeffersonian Republicanism to Federalism and then to conservatism and republicanism. Some Federalists, however, were New England based free traders. Clay's arguments and the rise of American manufacturing won over many Federalists who believed in the destiny of the American republic as a world power. One of the most important New England converts was Daniel Webster. Clay and Webster had grown up in the economic debates between the Jeffersonians and the Federalists over the national Bank. The Whigs also supported the National Bank, which President Jackson opposed so forcibly. Their support of the National bank was rooted in the need for available credit for manufacturing. A national bank would be operated for the good of the nation. Today, private banks are the biggest supporters of free trade because they make more money with trade than national manufacturing.

Henry Clay pulled together the anti-Jackson segment of bank supporters and built on the textile workers of New England to unite with his middle states support. Henry Clay toured the textile industry several times in the 1830s to further promote his "American System." One of the mills was named after Henry Clay to honor his protective tariffs. Even Clay's enemy, Andrew Jackson, honored the textile industry with a personal tour. Clay was now able to address the hero of free trade and the Democrats' philosophical heart — Adam Smith. Adam Smith's 1776 book, *Wealth of Nations*, had become the banner for free trade. Henry Clay now argued that free trade could reduce prices in the short run but at the expense of capital investment, invention, and automation. Furthermore, Clay saw capitalism as a national philosophy, not an attribute of free trade and internationalism. Still, the farming majority saw it much differently, fearing international reprisals and higher prices for domestic crops, if America put tariffs on incoming product.

The counter-revolution of Clay and Daniel Webster resulted in an alliance between labor and capital under protectionism, which would be embodied in the formation of the Whig party and later the Republican Party. Clay believed the laborer to be part of American capitalism. This fundamental premise of an alliance of labor and capital and the strength of that alliance would define the success of the new Whig party as well as the Republican Party for the next 60 years. Laborers and mill workers also realized the annual pay depended on eliminating long layouts due to recessions and plant closings more than wage rate or strikes. To counter the 1820s folk hero, Andrew Jackson, the Whigs elected their own Scotch-Irish hero, Davy Crockett of Tennessee, to Congress. The Whigs would also attract future leaders such as Abe Lincoln, James Garfield, and Scotch-Irish William McKinley in the 1850s. This idea of an alliance between labor and capital did not assume two distinct classes but realized that America offered upward mobility not known in Europe. The original Republican view of Abe Lincoln was: "the interests of labor and capital were identical, because equality of opportunity in American society generated a social mobility which assured that today's laborer would be tomorrow's capitalist." Upward mobility was the fuel of the capitalistic engine; without it, we would have a feudal system, socialism, and/or aristocracy established by birth.

Clay's American System tariffs had funded thousands of miles of canals and roads. The American System had expanded the iron, glass, textile, forging, casting, lumber, and meat industries. Tariffs were, of course, central to the Whig Party, which were opposed by the farmers in the Democratic Party as well as the union leadership. In the breakup of the Whig Party over slavery, the pro-slavery Whigs formed the Republican Party, running ex-Whig Abe Lincoln as their presidential candidate. The ex-Whigs dominated the early Republican Party, reinforcing the use of protectionism. Since the Whig party had been based on economic development, major social issues like slavery readily fractured it. The Protestant based Whigs further promoted the return of profits to society through philanthropy, which became capitalism's response to the socialism of Europe. They expanded colleges and schools on the state level. They argued that a healthy American economy was the medicine for many of the nation's social ills.

To focus solely on the political ramifications of Clay's American System, however, would also be to overlook the realization of Clay's (and ultimately McKinley's) dream of an Industrial Eden. And it truly was a system where tariffs were focused to help infant industries; and the tariff revenues were used to build roads and canals. In the Northeast, textile mills were growing; in Pennsylvania and Ohio, iron furnaces were being built; and the American nation was moving from an underdeveloped country to an industrialized one in the first decade of the 1800s. The heart of the Whig Party was in the manufacturing districts of New England's textile industry, the iron industry of Ohio and Pennsylvania, and western mining districts in Illinois and Michigan (today's Rust Belt). In Ohio and Western Pennsylvania, the Whigs were known as the Pig Iron Aristocracy because of the iron manufacturer's financial support of the party. Even industrial critics such as Charles Dickens were holding the American system of industrialization up as utopian. The manufacturing methods and automation of American industry were rapidly becoming the standard of efficiency for the world. Pioneering American industrialists such as Francis Cabot Lowell started to develop uniquely American textile factories. While still physically demanding, the factories were clean and offered schooling and training. Even old Jeffersonians were proud of the rise of American manufacturing supremacy.

Southerners such as Thomas Jefferson and James Madison, of the then Democratic-Republican Party of the time, were the Whigs' opposition. The South feared retaliation for tariffs on their exports of cotton and tobacco. The division would remain and would be the root cause of the Civil War. The Hamilton tariff was to be a moderate one of more use in raising money for the government than full protection. The more hotly debated part of Hamilton's plan was government subsidies direct to manufacturers. Most argued for indirect subsidies such as the building of roads and canals. Even manufacturers preferred a high tariff for protection versus government subsidies which might lead to political favoritism. It would be President William McKinley that gave capitalism the one thing it lacked — a national mission. McKinley the politician also understood that the alliance of the workers and plant owners was a powerful political coalition (one that made him one of the country's most popular presidents ever).

McKinley's Bill of 1890 is discussed above in Chapter 2 and elsewhere. First, McKinley argued that the revenue tariff approach was the real problem, not protective tariffs. His statistics were convincing: "Before 1820 nearly all our imports were dutiable; scarcely any were free; while in 1824 the proportion of free imports was less than 6 percent; in 1830, about 7 percent.... The percent of free imports from 1873 to 1883 was about 30 percent, and under the tariff revision of 1883 it averaged 33 percent." For his 1890 bill, it would be 50 percent. The difference was that it focused on the nation's industrial needs, not on revenue producing (for years, tariffs had been the only major source of government income). The plan was fully consistent with the Federalists' and the Whigs' views of a manufacturing utopia.

Interestingly, Big Banking was the major opposition to McKinley's ideas. The big bankers divided the old Republican Party from its more populist roots. It also divided Big Business, which supported tariffs, from Big Banking. In the McKinley era, the big New York banks did not have full control yet. Regional banks like Mellon Bank in Pittsburgh supplied the needed capital for the steel and the aluminum industry.

As President, McKinley pushed for reciprocity arrangements through treaties in the 1897 Dingley tariff. Debated at the time, reciprocity gave protectionist America a perception of fairness. Many conservatives were concerned that McKinley's reciprocity arrangements would lead to an erosion of protectionism, but McKinley believed it was necessary for the future. American surplus was becoming an issue, and McKinley wanted to allow for a boom in exports. In his last speech at Buffalo, McKinley defined his vision: "A system which provides a mutual exchange of commodities is manifestly essential to continued and healthful growth of our export trade. . . Reciprocity is the natural outgrowth of our wonderful industrial development under the domestic policy now firmly established . . . The expansion of our trade and commerce is a pressing problem. Commercial wars are unprofitable. A policy of good will and friendly trade relations will prevent reprisals. Reciprocity treaties are in harmony with the spirit of the times; measures of retaliation are not." Reciproc-

ity was how McKinley avoided the dreaded cries of Mont Pèlerin economists that tariffs would lead to trade wars and depression.

Statistics for the 1890 to 1900 decade support the conclusion of
McKinley's success that prices came down, profits rose, capital investment went up, and wages held or slightly increased (real wages clearly
rose). Even more important, American wages and benefits were the highest in the industrialized world. Average annual manufacturing income
went from $425.00 a year and $1.44 a day in 1890 to $432.00 a year and
$1.50 a day in 1900. The average day in manufacturing remained around
10 hours a day. Heavily protected industries such as steel fared slightly
better with wages. The cost of living index fell during the decade from 91
to 84, or about 8 percent. The clothing cost of living dropped even more
from 134 to 108, or 19 percent. Food stayed about the same, but the cost
of protected sugar dropped around 25 percent. The bottom line is that
real wage (adjusted for cost of living) index rose from $1.58 a day to $1.77
a day in 1900, or about a 12 percent increase. Invention flowered during
the period as companies invested in research and development to meet
congressional oversight of profits.

The success of this period of managed trade depended on government
oversight, business cooperation, and labor support. The list of companies
that built their foundation and expanded included Libbey Glass, United
States Steel, Standard Oil, ALCOA, H.J. Heinz (there was a 40 percent
tariff on pickles), and Bethlehem Steel, to name a few. Most importantly,
America believed in itself and industry, unions, and the government were
united in the dominance of America. It was the very type of economic
nationalism that the Mont Pèlerin Society blamed the world problems
on. The McKinley era was one that was not mentioned in the early meetings of the Mont Pèlerin Society.

Another lost concept of Hamilton, Clay, the Whigs, and McKinley
was the use of protection to support infant and new industries against
foreign economic attack. Protection of struggling industries is much
cheaper for government in the long run. McKinley gave capitalism a type
of national direction without the central planning of communism and
socialism. Free trade has cost the United States its standing in the world.
Yet government continues to spend endlessly to cover the private losses
caused by de-industrialization while holding to free trade for the bankers. Meanwhile, McKinley's ideas are far from forgotten; in fact, they are
very much being applied in Beijing.

Since the American people and government cannot interpret what is
happening, is there any hope? De-industrialization kills by many small

cuts. Maybe the federal government will wake up as our national debt skyrockets, our workers become welfare dependents and our lack of industry fuels purchasing from China and increases national debt. Maybe as the politicians feel the pain, things will change. The other hope is that much of the rust belt is still a gold mine of personal energy and ingenuity, which may lead to re-industrialization. Business, communities, and politicians need to come together to make it work. Maybe we need a new meeting on the hills, this time overlooking the great Mon Valley. And maybe we need to dig up the old Whig party.

TIMELINE

1977. Black Monday September 19 — Youngstown Sheet & Tube closes Youngstown plant

1978. Youngstown's United States Steel and Jones & Laughlin Plants close

1983. USS Homestead and Carrie Furnaces in Mon Valley closed

1990. Saturn opens

1999. Buick Assembly Flint Plant closes

Bibliography

Bluestone, Barry and Bennett Harrison. *The De-industrialization of America*. New York: Basic Books, 1982.

Buckley, William F. Jr., *Let Us Talk of many Things: The Collected Speeches*. Basic Books: New York, 2006.

Cumbler, John T. *A Social History of Economic Decline*. New Brunswick: Rutgers University Press, 1989.

Dyer, Joyce. *Gum-Dipped: A Daughter Remembers Rubber Town*. Akron: University of Akron Press, 2003.

Eisler, Bentia, The Lowell Offering: Writings by New England Mill Women. New York: W. W. Norton, 1998.

Ford, Henry. *My Life and Times*. New York: Doubleday, 1924.

Hall, Christopher. *Steel Phoenix: The Fall and Rise of the U.S. Steel Industry*. New York: St. Martin's Press, 1997.

Halberstam, David. *The Reckoning*, New York: Avon Books, 1987.

Hayek, Friedrich. *The Road to Serfdom: The Definitive Edition*. Chicago: University of Chicago Press, 2007.

Hoerr, John. And The Wolf Finally Came: Decline of the American Steel Industry. Pittsburgh: University of Pittsburgh, 1988.

Hogan, William T. *The 1970s: Critical Years for Steel*. Lexington: Lexington Books, 1972.

Hogan, William T. *World Steel in the 1980s*. Lexington: Lexington Books, 1983.

Linkon, Sherry Lee and John Russo, *Steel-Town U.S.A.* Lawrence: University of Kansas Press, 2002.

MacArthur, John. *The Selling of Free Trade: NAFTA, Washington and Subversion of American Democracy*. Berkeley: University of California Press, 2001.

MacArthur, John. "The De-industrialization of America," *Counterpunch*, August 5, 2011.

Miner, Curtis. *Homestead: The Story of a Steel Town*. Pittsburgh: Historical Society of Western Pennsylvania, 1989.

Modell, Judith. *A Town Without Steel: Envisioning Homestead*. Pittsburgh: University of Pittsburgh Press, 1998.

Skousen, Mark. *Vienna & Chicago: Friends or Foes?* Washington: Capital Press, 2006.

Skrabec, Quentin. *The Boys of Braddock*. Westminster: Heritage Books, 2004.

Taylor, Alex. *Sixty to Zero: An Inside Look at the Collapse of General Motors and the Detroit Auto Industry*. New Haven: Yale University Press, 2010.

Warren, Kenneth. *Big Steel: The First Century of United States Corporation*. Pittsburgh: University of Pittsburgh Press, 2003.

Wapshott, Nicholas. *Keynes Hayek: The Clash That Defined Modern Economics*. New York: W. W. Norton & Company, 2011

Wymard, Ellie. *Talking Steel Towns: The Men and Women of America's Steel Valley*. Pittsburgh: Carnegie-Mellon Press, 2007.

Yates, Brock. *The Decline & Fall of the American Automobile Industry*. New York: Vintage Books, 1984.

INDEX

74326239R00131

Made in the USA
Columbia, SC
01 August 2017